Tennessee Tears

By
George John Curtis

with
Ira L. White

SECOND EDITION
ISBN 0-9658302-09
TENNESSEE TEARS

Table of Contents
DEDICATION
INTRODUCTION
PREFACE

PART ONE
LIFE AS BRIAN

PART TWO
LIFE AS GEORGE

BIBLIOGRAPHY

DEDICATED TO

Mr. Robert Mathias
A Champion of Champions
And
To the memory of the
deceased victims of the
Tennessee Children's Home Society
Scandal whose lives had true meaning

INTRODUCTION

The largest black market baby selling scandal in American history is forty-five years behind us. So why is it just now getting the massive media coverage it should have gotten on September 13, 1950, when it was first exposed?

Many forces, primarily negative, suppressed it for their own gain and protection. Thousands of families could have been reunited if the right thing had been done. Politicians who feigned ignorance of the scandal were in essence furthering their own careers on the blood and sweat of thousands of innocent children. Since that time the order of things has been askew. The Tennessee Children's Home Society Scandal wasn't the only scandal, just the largest. How many more scandals are lurking in the dark waiting to be discovered? It is time to put order back in the adoption process.

Unfortunately, conditions have changed little in the fifty years since the scandal. Children are still at risk, still being treated with indifference to their human rights. From a historical viewpoint, when major advances have been achieved in a particular area, e.g., Civil Rights and Martin Luther King Jr.; Susan B. Anthony and the rights of women; Senator Claude Pepper and elderly rights; Dennis Means and

Indian rights; a special person who is closely (usually on a personal level) related to that cause, emerges to lead the fight.

The Adoption Reform Movement (ARM) needs such a champion. Someone who has been directly affected by adverse conditions to the point where his entire existence is consumed and devoted toward the betterment of his fellowman is a true altruist.

Many times I have wondered what would have happened if I hadn't been a victim of the Tennessee Children's Home Society Scandal. But if I hadn't, then all of the wonderful things that are occurring now wouldn't have been possible.

I was not brought into this world to become the champion of adoption reform. Or was I? If it turns out that way, I will be proud to carry the mantle of responsibility.

This book with a plethora of reasons in mind. I have massaged all of these reasons and culled the most important one - I had to. The story revealed is one that can be an example to untold numbers who still suffer from missing their own identities. It is the story of just one of thousands of precious children denied their birthrights.

The "Right to Know Movement" is gaining wider support because, unlike our childhood days, thousands of us are now adults with voices that will not be beaten into submission. The politicians will not turn their backs this time. Without the caring and action of the "Right to Know Movement", I would still be wandering in the wilderness.

Adoption reform is a major issue today. The numerous scandals that have been exposed over the past several decades are unavoidable examples of this nation's callous treatment of her young.

Whether in news reports or in television specials, adoption reform is being fed, in a major way, to Americans. The need is so great, that society is finally being forced to address the issue.

There are numerous pros and cons on the adoption reform issue. My only answer is that God's laws come before man's laws. No man has the right to deny another man what is rightfully his - his family. Demagoguery needs to be permanently retired.

I had a dream and I lived it. I now have new dreams to take the place of those come true. My ultimate dream is that not a single child be put through hell like I was.

I never dreamed that I would write a book. My dreams never went further than finding my family. I had no purpose in life - I do now. Only one element is missing to complete the necessary equation so that the adoption reform movement completes its appointed goal of Leadership.

I have given my respects to many loving people in the text. Ira White deserves a great amount of respect for his patience with me. I stretched his rubber band to the limits and it didn't snap. Thanks, Ira!

To my sister, Kathy, I owe the most. She has been the one constant that has kept my universe from falling off of Atlas' shoulders. My sincere appreciation to Connie Daniel for her many hours on her computer proofreading, correcting, and running copies on the printer; and to Clifford Ward for the many hours he spent with me on his computer doing the original printing. Also deserving my humble appreciation is Lani Nesbit, who's half hour interview on the Post-Newsweek weekly show, "Another Look", helped put further light on a dark chapter in America's history, but also a light on what needs to be done. My thanks to Marcella Dallas Fleming who edited this edition.

I didn't set out in life to be courageous. I did set out to discover the truth. Along the way, courage was my unknown companion. That and the prayers of my family, are what brought about "Tennessee Tears". I hope you, the reader, enjoy reading this miraculous story as much as I enjoyed living and writing it.

PREFACE

Business in Babies

It was December 1948.   Cold wind whipped across
the Memphis Municipal Airport while two women
waited for the flight to Nashville.   One woman was
the wife of Dr. Owen S. Gibbs and the other of city
engineer W.B. Fowler.

Nearby, a third woman cuddled two tiny babies.
Mrs. Gibbs and Mrs. Fowler chirped at the infants
and the woman explained that they were twins, bound
for New York and adoption. But the New York plane
was four hours late.

The two wives suggested that the babies be
taken to a warmer place to wait. Their guardian hur-
ried off to a phone booth and returned to say she had
called a taxi. So, when a big, black, chauffeur-driven
car arrived, instead of a cab, Mrs. Gibbs and Mrs.
Fowler jotted down the license number. The car, they
discovered later, belonged to Miss Georgia Tann,
executive secretary of the Memphis division of the
Tennessee Children's Home Society, a private, non-
profit institution occupying a mansion at 1556 Poplar Street.

To questioners, Miss Tann insisted the children were twins and that they were going to a couple
somewhere "this side of New York" who had ap-

plied for twins three years before. The children proved not to be twins. One was 12 days old, the other 23 days. They were going to separate families. The nurse's ticket was for New York. [Newsweek 10-02-50]

TO MOM

I love you
Whispered the cool evening breeze
From the lips of one
Who I would never meet
Gentle was her heart
That saw me come
Alas, not to see me go
She comes to me often
Through my dreams
Our hearts are one
Our dreams are what
We share spanning both
Time and eternity

Part 1: *Life as Brian*

CHAPTER ONE
Adopted

*And the child lifted his heart and soul up to
God on the wings of his beautiful young voice, need-
ing nothing but God as his audience. And the Lord
listened and drew the child to him.*

From early childhood, "I'm adopted," became
my battle cry. Many children are adopted into loving
homes where two people, unable to have their own
children, are thrilled to accept a child of God into
their family. To them the sound of children laughing
and running about is music that has been excluded
from their lives. They feel thankful for their adopted
children and treat them as if they were the fruits of
their own union. This is not so for some of us. It was
not so for me.

I can remember how special Sunday evenings
were to me when I was very young. "The Wonderful
World of Disney" was on television every Sunday
evening. Kathy, my fraternal sister, and I would be
on the floor like a couple of rug rats while Jon, my
adopted brother, sat between John and Doris, my
adopted parents, on the couch.

Tinker Bell would splash star dust across the

black and white TV screen, Jimminy Cricket would sing "When You Wish Upon A Star," and in a hidden place deep inside me, I wished that some day I could find my real parents. I would think, "What a terrible mistake—I'm not supposed to be here with these mean people." I knew in my heart that God was good and kept asking myself why He had put me here. I was unwanted by my adoptive parents. They told me they loved and wanted me, but their behavior and abusive actions toward me conveyed a different message. They let me know time and time again that I was adopted (You're going back to the orphanage if you don't straighten up!), so I sometimes had the feeling that my real parents didn't want me either. What was wrong with me?

My sister was wanted by our adoptive parents. She had been chosen by them to round out a perfect family: one successful father, one mother to keep the home, a blonde blue-eyed little boy, our adopted brother, and a cute little girl. Then there was me, the proverbial two for one child. I love my sister very much, but I doubt she understands what it is like to feel unwanted as a child. Though some of the cruelty to me also fell on her, despite her being a "wanted child", she never knew about many of the atrocities inflicted on me. In her teen years, sis had to deal with her own Hell.

Jon, the "Golden Child", had been adopted as

an infant from St. Peter's before my sister and I were. His treatment was special. He was put on a pedestal. I cannot remember his ever being a victim of corporal punished, for any incident of his. I was singled out for the rod, and even my sister had a taste of how it felt, but Jon's body went totally unscathed. He was, however, subject to verbal abuse. I never liked Jon, but I am glad that he was not brutalized. That is something no child should ever have to endure.

John William Bubnes, my adopted father, was born in Edinburgh, Scotland of Lithuanian stock. John was one of several children. I know of three sisters and two brothers.

At an early age his family immigrated to the United States through Ellis Island in New York where the family was asked for their name. The Americans misunderstood them, so the true family name, Urbanas, became Bubnes. God, how I hated that name!

John was a coal miner in Pennsylvania when he met and married Doris Maud Brown. Sometime during their marriage, which lasted thirty-eight years, they separated for a period of time. During their separation, Doris took up with a boxer, Harold Dugas. When John and Doris finally divorced in 1968, she moved back to Detroit, Michigan and Harold. This event coincided with my entry into the Air Force.

During World War II, John served as a Mess

Sergeant. I remember playing with his old army gear as a child. After the war, John, with the help of Doris' parents, opened up a butcher shop and grocery store in Detroit. He worked hard, and by the time I was adopted, he owned a flourishing business.

Doris Maud Brown is now eighty years old. If John were alive, he would be eighty something. John and Doris were about forty when they adopted Kathy, my older sister, and me. I draw your attention to their ages, because in my adult years I have observed people who became grandparents in there mid to late thirties. John and Doris were old enough to be our grandparents when they adopted us. By the time I was ten, they were fifty. Not once do I remember John playing football, baseball or any other game with me.

Doris, my adopted mother, was an only child. Her parents were from England. They were exceptionally nice people who treated me with more respect and dignity than their daughter and son-in-law. Wherever you are Grandma and Grandpa, I love you and thank you.

Physically, Doris was a beautiful woman. John used to tell me how she was so slender when young that he could put his hands around her waist. By the end of their marriage, I think they would both like to have put their hands around each other's necks.

Kathy, my fraternal sister, was born June 4,

1948, in Bluefield, West Virginia. I have never met an individual who surpasses her compassion and understanding of animals. There is innocence about Kathy that unfortunately has been used against her by others throughout her life. The cruel advantage they have taken of her has hurt me severely, for I love her with all my heart. She is forty-five years old now, and people are still profiting from her innocence. I am happy that, even though she was taken advantage of, her innocence still survives a monument that testifies to her continued charm.

Kathy is also one of the most beautiful women walking the face of this earth. It would have been difficult for John and Doris to resist her lovely brown eyes and that cute pixie face with the sunny smiles that only hinted at the impishness hiding inside. They couldn't resist, and that is why they went shopping for one and came home with two.

I was a very small child, no older than four years, having been with John and Doris since I was about two, when something happened that is fixed in my memory forever. Before me in soup bowl was a mixture of cold rice pudding and my own vomit. I liked rice, so I didn't understand at the time what had caused me to throw up. As it turned out, I had an acute nervous stomach disorder brought on by stress.

John, my adopted father, jerked me from my

chair with one hand while scooping up the bowl and its contents with the other. Terrified and unable to escape his iron grip, I was hurled to the kitchen floor. I felt so small and so afraid. John reminded me of Goliath, and I was David. "When you're through with that bowl," bellowed Goliath, "I'm taking you back to the orphanage so you can live with the rest of the little bastards!"

I'm not sure which terrified me the most—the threat of being returned like a bag of defective merchandise, or Goliath towering over me ordering this small child of God to eat his own vomit. I also had a deep-seated fear of losing the only person in my life whom I truly loved, my sister. In my defense, I scrambled to Doris and attached myself to her leg pleading for clemency. This is a tactic I would use again in the future to save myself from being further brutalized by Goliath.

Sometimes I was not able to use this tactic. If I was in bed by the time John got home, I might be safe for the night. I would hear him tramp in and feel my heart begin to pound. Then the drinking would start. Lying in bed awake, trembling and listening to John and Doris begin the evening ritual of yelling at each other, I would strain to hear the conversation to see if my name was mentioned. If it was, I could expect to hear John stomp down the hallway knowing that, after the door burst open, I would be yanked

out of bed and either beaten with his fists or, on special occasions, dragged into his bedroom, stripped
of my pajamas and whipped with his belt.

Some nights I would actually be asleep when
suddenly a red-faced Goliath who would then beat
me would rip me from my dreams. I wonder what
my sister, Kathy, thought while this was going on. I
know sometimes I was wishing that it were she receiving the beatings instead of me. But when she
took her own licks, it didn't make me feel any better.

There were other nights when I would vomit
in my bed in anticipation of the coming festival of
abuse. When this happened, I would try to hide the
vomit. If John saw it when he came to give me my
due, he would be even more enraged than normal.
All I can say is that my poor Teddy was never the
same after these episodes began.

Jon never had to worry. He had Doris to protect him. She would hold court when John came
home, sitting in her chair with her knitting in her lap
(she was an excellent knitter) and a highball standing neatly on a coaster on the table beside her chair.
Jon played the court favorite while she solemnly
served up an accounting of the day's indiscretions,
meted out her judgment and dispatched the execu-
tioner to do his work. Jon would snicker under his
breath at the end of these proceedings, just loud
enough for me to notice. The strap wasn't all that

burned my butt.

On my tenth birthday I had a birthday party. Jon carried the cake from the kitchen to the carport where we were having the party. When he got close enough for me to see him clearly, he plopped the cake upside down on the sidewalk and flashed me a wicked smile. The Golden Child never got in trouble for this and was given all sorts of sympathy because he might have hurt himself.

Another time I was playing down the street minding my own business, when I suddenly felt something hit my hand. At first I thought it was a bee sting, but the welt on my hand did not look like a bee sting. Then I noticed Jon standing further up the road with his trusty Springfield BB rifle, smiling stupidly. I raced home and told Doris what had happened. She called Jon into the house and told him not to shoot at me again. I was flabbergasted. I knew I would have caught hell had I done the same thing.

I went on playing as I had before feeling a bit cheated. A little while later I felt another stinging sensation. I ran home again and complained to Doris that he had shot me again. When confronted with my accusations, Jon told Doris that he had not shot at me. He had shot at the asphalt road and the BB ricocheted into my behind. He wasn't even put on probation.

Jon was not immune to our adopted father's

anger. He grew up with, what I believe to be a stomach disorder from listening to Kathy and me get beat up and berated. The stomach problems are symptomatic of a larger nervous disorder. His hands are so unsteady that I am sure he has trouble putting the dipstick into its hole when he checks the oil of customers at the service station where he works. He was also shouted at, but John dared not touch one hair on his head. Oh, how well John wanted to take a swipe at this little boy as well. Each time he was thwarted by the evil eye of Doris and had to walk away shaking his head in total frustration. The loss of absolute control was like a knife twisting in his gut.

Doris was quick with a smile for every one— every one except me. I never bonded with her psychologically. I tried to gain her love, but her love was for no one except my adopted brother Jon, the Golden Child. All too many times, I have observed men who make fools of themselves trying to secure the love of their mothers, mothers who loved their other children more. It is a truly pathetic sight, one that I share with other unfortunate ones. The habit of attempting to secure love from unreciprocating mothers carries on into adulthood with the women chosen to pursue for marriage. Constant low self-esteem permeates the process. Thus, I have been attracted to many beautiful women who have treated me the same way Doris did. Since the process works for both genders, my sister was also affected. Her three divorces, from men who treated her terribly, attests to this.

Doris was always wearing clothes several sizes too small for her. She shopped often and usually took me along. I disliked going, due to the beatings I would receive when John came home and Doris told him of the trouble I had caused. I had the uncanny knack of getting lost while in the local stores, a practice that earned me many a bruise when John was informed. Perhaps I was unconsciously searching for my real family. Doris eventually put me in a body harness. I was then trotted from store to store more like a dog than a family member.

When Doris and I went shopping, we always wound up in the women's lingerie department where Doris was always buying girdles packaged in long round tubes. I swore that when I grew up I would never set foot in another women's lingerie department. Well, no sooner did I get married to my first wife than I found myself once again led through the women's lingerie department! I'm not quite sure what the problem is. Lingerie has never been a problem in other circumstances!

Doris was a high school graduate, and her husband was an elementary school dropout. Despite these facts, they were well off. Besides two homes, one on Prevost Street in Detroit, Michigan and the other on Bogie Lake, they owned an adjacent lot next

to the house on Prevost. They drove brand new cars,
and had the services of a maid, Ardella, a sweet,
portly, black woman, and a handyman named Barney.
There was private school for Kathy and me; mem-
bership in the John L. Ivory Polo Club; trips to Florida
every winter (Jon would go on the trips but Kathy
and I were left behind at Grandma's); and Royal
Dalton China to adorn the dining tables in both
homes. John would donate large amounts of food
for events at Immaculate Heart fund-raisers. He was
also a personal friend of J. Mennen Williams, Governor of Michigan. Last, but not least, there was the
quarter horse, Ford.

One might wonder why I was given private
school and Jon was sent to public school. Believe
me, it does not show a willingness to make up for
loss of favoritism in other areas. I was sent to private
school because my behavior was so anti-social the
public schools would not have me. Anyone surprised
by this admission does not know the world of abused
children. Children of alcoholics have a similar reaction in their struggle to cope with a world that even
to a child seems out of whack. There are two roads
for these children to travel: they may become overly
responsible and take the world on their shoulders or
they become totally irresponsible troublemakers. The
overly responsible child earns high marks for behavior and his work in school. The irresponsible child is

the opposite. What they both have in common is the damage they have suffered. One is eaten alive from the inside out—the other from the outside in.

I was adopted into, and raised in, an abusive alcoholic family. In addition, I was continually under the threat of losing the family I had. There were times when John actually jumped in the car with me and began to drive off to the orphanage where I could live with the rest of the little bastards. I might have welcomed that happening if it were not for the fact that both John and Doris pummeled me with how they had rescued me from a life of evil at the orphanage. There was also a feeling of terror over and above the apprehension of losing my adopted family. Some forgotten memory was associated with my stay at the orphanage. Were it not for this memory instilling terror in dusty corners of my mind and the loss of my sister, I would not have been affected by John and Doris' threats to send me back. I might even have challenged them to go ahead and send me back. Years later I would solve the mystery of the forgotten memory and uncover another mystery in the process.

There was one instance when John became my protector. I lived in a fantasy world most of the time. Superman, Tarzan, and Robin Hood were my constant companions. I still identify with Peter Pan. We were both lost boys, orphans who never wanted to

grow up. I called my fantasy world Sherwood Forest and was playing there when the Sheriff of
Naughty, an older boy in the neighborhood, sexually
molested me.

I streaked home, terrified. John was already "
three sheets to the wind". He went off like a rocket
when he heard what I said. He snatched me up, and
we flew out the door. I didn't know what to expect. I
figured I was in trouble again, because the old man
had the crazed look in his eyes that he would get
when it was time for a good thrashing.

An argument ensued at the boy's house. I never
saw the boy again. I have often listened to other
adults, abused as children, relate how their steppar-
ents protected them from the abuse of others. It's
almost like they are saying, "If this child is going to
be abused, it will be kept in the family".

Doris was not innocent when it came to dish-
ing out physical abuse. One time I was playing with
the knobs on the kitchen stove. Doris discovered me
doing the forbidden thing, and being the voyeur of
physical punishment that she was, instructed Ardella,
our maid, to turn on the electric burners and place
my hands on them. Ardella, as I have said before,
was a sweet lady. In the past she had been quick to
follow my adopted parents' instructions, knowing
that to please the boss was to keep the job. In this
case, however, she refused, and strongly objected.

Doris was forced by her sick mind to do the deed herself.

"Leave It to Beaver," was a favorite television program for millions of Americans. I didn't buy it. When Beaver got into trouble Ward, his father, never smacked him around. Mrs. Cleaver was also too incredibly sweet to be genuine and too understanding to have ever dealt with the real world. Now I enjoy watching reruns of the program because they seem so absurd to me, they make me laugh. One of my favorite lines from the show is when June Cleaver says to her husband, "Weren't you a little hard on the Beaver last night, Ward?"

Even though Kathy is fourteen months older than I am, we were placed in the same grade at Immaculate Heart School in Detroit. I was told that Kathy had a mental problem, a fact I had already come to believe based on her inability to articulate properly. Several of the same cruel children who made fun of my braces and eye patches and called me a bastard informed me that my sister was retarded. In reality, every one was wrong. Kathy only had a speech problem, which is understandable due to the circumstances.

While working on my Masters Degree in Special Education, I learned that many children who had speech problems were the victims of early childhood trauma. A typical child speaks in sentences comprised

of a number of words that parallel the age of the child.
For instance, a four-year-old will speak in four word
sentences. When Kathy was adopted at about four
years of age, she was only capable of articulating
the phrase, "Dada." The trauma that impaired her
ability to learn speech had to have occurred prior to
her adoption. Probably during her stay at St. Peter's
Orphanage. Perhaps with some further investigation,
I will be able to solve this mystery as well.

My sister and I got along for the most part.
There were, however, several instances of her being
uncommonly mean to me. In one case, she threw a
dart at me. The dart pierced my ear and came close
to doing some permanent damage. I threw the dart
back at her and stuck her in the leg for retribution.
She also used to pull me under the water when we
were swimming and not let me come up. After I had
fought to the surface and struggled free of her grasp,
she would laugh at me. I still loved her. She wouldn't
let other kids abuse me in any way. On several occasions, she beat up bigger kids for being mean to me.
This is similar to the way John reacted to the kid
who molested me. Kathy was abused herself and as
a result she abused me, the littlest one in the family.
And how did I react when the only one in this world,
whom I felt truly loved me, also abused me? When I
thought I could get away with it, I retaliated by blam-
ing her for things I did that would get me in trouble.

I remember one incident, when I was six years old, of Kathy being mean to me. I was confused about it until just recently. We were playing on the playground at Immaculate Heart School in Detroit. Kathy coerced all the kids to sing the old nursery rhyme, "Georgie Porgie Puddin' Pie," to me. They nearly drove me crazy. She was four when we were adopted, and had remembered my given name. All I knew was that I was Brian.

The "normal" children called me other names, as I grew up. The most damaging of these was bastard!

In the fifties, it was almost a crime to be a child born out of wedlock. If you were adopted, most other kids assumed this was the case and stuck you with the label. The "normals" got this from their parents who were outraged that two people could have sex without being married and who stupidly assumed that all children at orphanages were bastards. My status as an adopted child was well known by my classmates. I never heard the end of it. I was not one to allow such despoiling of my name. Consequently, I regularly went a round or two with some of the "normal" kids who insisted on referring to me as a bastard. I wanted desperately to find my family so I would no longer have to deal with this horrible name. Now there are so many children of questionable origin that the word, "bastard", has lost its impact. Still,

I have made sure that the children I fathered have my name.

During the fifties there was another form of abuse visited upon other children and myself. Children in some nursery schools were made to wear clothespins on their body parts for unacceptable behavior. I would walk around with clothespins attached to my nose, lips, ears and fingers looking a little like a Christmas tree. It was all legal, of course. This was an acceptable deterrent to antisocial behavior designed to "teach" the perpetrator a lesson. What lesson do you think all of us little anti-socials really learned?

The seed of desire to find my biological family found little nourishment in those early years. What started as a dream, watching Disney, received lots of negative motivation. Each time I felt the welts growing on my young bottom, each time I was clobbered with fists, felt the plunger or broom handle exploding on my tender flesh, I became more resolved to unearth my true family roots.

The first piece of information I ferreted out of Doris was a result of the following question: "Why did you go all the way to Tennessee to adopt me?" Doris's reply was that there had been a baby kidnapping ring in Michigan, so they were forced to go to Tennessee to adopt me. The way she said it made me feel like they had gone to great extremes to adopt me, and because of their extreme efforts, I should be even more grateful.

A few years later, a second piece of information fell into my life like a paste jewel dropped into a highwayman's bag. Doris alleged that my biological mother, after having signed the surrender papers on my sister and me, changed her mind. She supposedly returned to the orphanage, kidnapped me and took off for Chicago.

As the story goes, she was arrested in Chicago, and I was returned to St. Peter's.

With just these two pieces of information to hold on to, I spent forty years in the wilderness of life with only hope and my fantasies to nourish my soul. For years the seed planted within me grew with my fantasies, and the horrors of my life would be temporarily obliterated by an imagined last minute rescue by my mother, the good fairy, or my father, every bit as swashbuckling as Erroll Flynn. When I began to drink at an early age, however, the tree grown from this seed withered in the face of a drought that lasted for many years after the poison of alcohol had left my system. It lasted until a kind friend poured a drink of sweet spring water around the roots of the tree and green shoots again appeared. Mom, Dad, did you love me? Mom, Dad, where are you now?

CHAPTER TWO
Polio

My last vaccination for polio was while I was still at St. Peter's. According to my health records, the doctor there discovered I carried the polio virus. I don't know how young I was, but I was very small, when I first visited the clinic. Every one around me was wearing white. The hot lights blared down on me. I also remember the big room where a large group of people mingled.

A few chairs away from me sat a little girl. Her presence made me feel uneasy. I swiveled my head to get a better look at her and had the hell scared out of me. Her eyes were like those of a gargoyle. Something about her body seemed unnatural, ugly. She just kept staring at me. Her terrible eyes bored into me until she impressed my young mind so vividly, I am able to recall, even today, the emotions that coursed through me. I doubt she was as scary as I thought, but at the time I was afraid she was the devil here on earth sent to fetch me to the fiery pits. I doubt that my perception was real. I was only about three years old when the incident occurred. But the emotions I experienced at the time were real enough.

After a long wait with my fear, I was ushered into a room with even brighter lights. Several machines were attached to me to measure the electrical impulses of my small soma. Rolls of lined paper spewed out from the machines. A long metal pen attached to each machine marched up and down the paper scratching zigzag lines onto its surface. At the time I didn't know how much these lines meant to me. They seemed simply a strange way of drawing funny pictures. I was also given a spinal tap at this time. Those of you who have had one, know how much fun they are. My conscious mind has forgotten the pain, but the unconscious never forgets.

The fear inspired by the young girl was short lived. I soon came to enjoy the attention I was receiving. I was honored. Angels in white hovered around me bestowing upon me more attention than I had ever received. My legs were gently and firmly pulled and the muscles were massaged. I imagined I had turned into a prince and relished the presence of these beings in white. Little did I realize these shinning white angels were fighting to save my life. The physical therapists were doing all they could to prevent my leg muscles from atrophying. I would like to thank these people who worked so hard to help me. It would be nice to be able to repay them for their efforts. But how do you repay someone for saving your life?

I visited the clinic daily and each time received a big lollipop. How I loved those lollipops, but I also loved the sound of, "What a brave boy you are!" Fall-

ing from the lips of the angel who supplied me with
these delicious treats. Eventually, I was fitted with
heavy steel braces. I only wore them for a brief period of time, but it was long enough for the taunts of
other children to be etched into my mind. My legs
did atrophy. To this day, one leg is smaller than the
other.

I was not aware that polio had reached epidemic proportions in this country. I was too young
to notice. Hospital wards throughout the United
States were equipped with iron lungs. Thousands of
people died as a result of this affliction of the central
nervous system. Those who survived were permanently affected, many to the point of being disabled.

I have known several people who have been
victims of polio. One of them, a polio victim too,
lived across from our home in Modesto, California.
Kathy has always been a beautiful girl. She was a
schoolteacher for many years and is currently working on her counseling credential at a local college.
Polio affected Kathy more than it has affected me.
She is now battling post polio syndrome. She is not
alone. All of us who survived polio continue to face
the possibility of post polio syndrome.

God bless Dr. Jonas Salk. He developed the
vaccine against polio that has saved many lives and
prevented others from living as cripples. His work
saved my life. But I live with the fear that the virus

can reclaim me and cripple me again or even kill me. If it does, I will be grateful for the time I have had, a time I have used to achieve a lifelong dream.

As a young adolescent who had to deal with polio, I empathized readily with others who had developed difficulties with their legs. Bob Mathias was one of them. I was inspired by his biography, which I read when I was ten. His legs were afflicted with a severe case of rickets, as a young man, so badly the doctors who treated him believed he would never walk again.

Bob Mathias never gave up. Neither did his mother. Against all odds he cloaked himself in the armor of loving care provided by his mother and friends and fought back. Every day his mother spent hour after hour administering physical therapy to his legs to keep them from atrophying. She was indeed a dedicated and a loving person.

Bob Mathias, from a little town called Tulare, approximately one hundred fifty miles south of my present home in Modesto, California, developed into a world class athlete. In 1948, and again in 1952, he won a gold medal in the Olympic Decathlon, a competition that is rated as the most grueling of sporting events.

I have the greatest respect for Bob Mathias. The respect is not for overcoming his handicap as much as for what he did with his life afterwards. The true benchmark of an individual's success is how they behave after the smoke of the battle has drifted away. Mr. Mathias did not stop at his gold medals. He went on to become a respected United States Congressman. His greatest gift to others and myself was his gift of hope and inspiration. I've never forgotten that treasure.

Writing this has caused me to recall the impression left on me by his biography. I have drawn strength from his example most of my life. Now I hope to repay the gems I withdrew from that treasure chest of love with my story. It is my hope that those with trouble in their lives will read my book and use my example to overcome the roadblocks to bettering themselves.

Besides polio, my vision problems as a child were acute. I believe I spent as much time in eye clinics as I spent in the polio clinic. Several doctors were consulted. The problem was finally diagnosed as weak eye muscle syndrome. One eye was weak. The good eye valiantly tried to compensate for the weak one causing my eyes to gravitate towards my nose. I was in the process of becoming cross-eyed.

The doctors prescribed a patch for the good eye to correct the condition. The idea was to force the weak eye muscles to work until they were built up enough to operate in tandem with the strong eye muscles. The doctors' prognosis was correct, and their remedial solution was successful. The doctors found that even with my weak eye corrected, I was still unable to correctly read the charts, and so I continue to wear glasses even today. The glasses hurt my eyes and many pairs were lost or broken. Beatings were administered each time my glasses were broken or lost.

The years of abuse on my little body and mind caused several psychological disorders to take on physical manifestations. When I was ten years old, I was still wetting the bed at night. Picture, if you will, a ten-year-old boy wearing a diaper made from a large bath towel. I remember having to fasten the large safety pins into the diaper myself. Jon, while in the presence of Doris, used to laugh at me. He was smart enough to know that doing this while alone with me would result in me heaping a helping of physical punishment on his plate. He had a habit of provoking me into physical action and then smirking as he watched me get beat.

In the following years I was eventually able to stop wetting the bed. Bed-wetting was replaced by a sleeping disorder. No matter how hard I tried, I couldn't get to sleep. Now the groundwork was laid for the use of alcohol as a sleeping aid.

Another disorder I developed was the vomiting. Experts in that era called it weak stomach. Psychologists now say that vomiting is a way for a child to get attention. Believe me. I did not want any more attention from John or Doris. Attention for me always meant pain. By the time I entered the service several years later, my vomiting was a major problem. My constant companions, Tums and Rolaids, would provide a little temporary relief. At age twenty I had myself checked out for ulcers. The doctors could find no physical reason for my stomach disorder. To this day, when the pressure is on, I still vomit. My alcoholism aggravated this problem.

I have learned that nature deals each one of us a different hand. Some of us have obviously received some bad hands. Others have been dealt a worse hand, even though it might appear they have the best cards to play. In a poker game, getting all the good cards may handicap a player, while the player dealt nothing but garbage might still bluff his way through. It is the same way in life. We can sit around feeling sorry for our bad luck or we can go out and do something about it. I choose to do something about it. The fun is not in the prize, it is in the chase to obtain it.

Chapter 3
The Good Times

Life has not always been bad. One day while
visiting our grandparents, the Browns, John pulled
up in front of their house in his new Buick. Jon and
Doris liked to show off the wealth they had accumulated, and the new Buick was one way of doing that.
John came into the house and told Jon to bring in the
box from the back seat of the car. Jon trotted in with
the box that he thought was empty except for a white
and tan calf skin rug rolled up at the bottom. When
he set the box down, the little ball of calfskin un-
rolled itself to reveal a collie puppy.

April was one of the rays of sunlight in my
life. She was officially given to Jon as a birthday
gift, but became the family pet for the next fourteen
years. Jon seldom took care of April. My sister and I
and Doris were the major caretakers of this wonderful little pup. For my part, a valuable lesson was
learned through April. I treated her with kindness
and care. In return she reflected all that love back to
me. As a result, I love animals. I have learned that if
you treat them with kindness, they return the favor.
It is unfortunate that all people cannot behave in this
same way.

There were times when I thought that April
received better treatment than I did. Doris would

chew Kraft Caramels for April. When the caramel was nice and soft, she would give it to her. Doris also bought specific cuts of meat for April. She would cook the meat, and then I would hand grind it. I thought this was an awful lot of work for a dog. The pangs of jealousy dug deep during these times. I should have been happy for April, and much of the time I was, because she was my buddy and confidant. She always listened patiently as privately I vocalized all those things I dared not speak aloud to anyone else.

When John was around, April would put her tail between her legs and run for cover. Even the family dog lived in fear of Goliath. I learned that one can usually tell what a person is like by watching their pet's reaction to them.

Doris' parents were from England and were very nice people who treated me with respect and dignity. Grandma Brown became one adult I could turn to for understanding and kindness. She also became my protector. Whenever John would turn into Goliath and the beating would begin, Grandma would scream at him to stop. When she cracked the whip, John always responded. I never understood the power she had over him, but Grandma, wherever you are, I love you.

Grandma Alice Brown, besides making me feel good about myself, was a good baker as many grandmothers used to be. I can clearly remember sitting in her kitchen, my mouth watering, as she rolled the dough for the sweetest pies and cookies in the universe. On the wall of her kitchen was a Bayer's Aspirin Calendar with a wealth of information about everyday things: when the sun rose, when it set, when the moon was new. She would always explain what the small round circles were, some half full, some full, some with just a sliver. Grandma was quick to teach. She would have been a superior teacher. A kinder, more caring person could not be found. We children spent a great deal of time at Grandma and Grandpa's where, thank goodness, we found peace.

In the evening, Grandma would plop Kathy and me into the bathtub together. The Golden Child took his own separate bath, so he missed out on the fun that we urchins shared with Grandma. Grandpa would be watching the fights sponsored by Gillette (If you want to look sharp and feel sharp, too) while Granny scrubbed us thoroughly with Fells Naphtha or Borax Twenty Mule Team. After we were a bright pink she would apply an ample coating of Johnson's Baby Powder. We were then put in our one-piece cotton flannel pajamas. After kissing every one good night, we were tucked into the most heavenly beds I can recall. Kathy and I would sleep in one bed and Jon in the other. When Grandma died, I lost a friend and protector, but not the memories of a kindly lady.

Grandpa Brown, I was informed by Doris, was a heavy drinker. He died at the age of seventy-one. The death certificate has the cause listed as pneumonia, but, in my opinion, the cause of death was cirrhosis. None of that matters to me now or mattered to me then, for Grandpa always treated me like most good grandfathers do—a pinch of cantankerousness and a full measure of love. His favorite nickname for me was "Barney." I'm not sure whether it was out of indifference to the name his daughter had chosen for me or because he couldn't remember the name Brian.

Grandpa Brown had retired from the Ford Motor Company of Detroit. Every payday he would give me a two dollar bill and several Hershey chocolate mini bars. Then he would take me for a bus ride around Detroit. He always made me feel special. I remember best the fishing trips we took together. He would usually sit and drink his six pack of beer and constantly complain about my fidgeting around in the boat that, he advised me, was scaring the fish away.

On one particularly memorable fishing trip I caught a nice three pound bass and attached it to the stringer slung over the side of the boat. I was so proud of myself and so was Grandpa. When we were still a half-mile out in the lake, Grandpa told me to start rowing the boat home. As we drew closer to our lakefront home, the landlubbers yelled out, as the custom was, "Did you catch anything?" When we were close enough, Grandpa told me to hold the fish up so those on shore could see our fine bass. I pulled the stringer out of the water keeping my eyes focused on catching the jealous reactions of the landlubbers. But something was wrong. The weight of the stringer wasn't as great as it should have been. I turned to look and was crushed to find that snapping turtles had eaten half of my beautiful bass. But I soon came to realize that Grandpa knew what a great catch it had been. Nothing else mattered.

The ranch style house we owned on Bogie Lake in the country was a favorite place of mine. When school was out, we used to stay there. The house was very nice, with plate glass windows stretching around the front and sides. There was a special place in the house for me. It was a built-in desk by a window that faced the neighbors' wall. I spent many hours there writing, "I am a bad boy." As a result, I have very good penmanship.

Thirty miles out of Detroit, the lake was definitely a major selling point for the place. Standing away from the water, the surrounding countryside was a forest of evergreens where one could hike and enjoy the natural surroundings. Down next to the lake were huge oak trees, perfect for climbing. The waters of Bogie Lake were filled with fish, frogs, turtles, and ducks. It was a great place to swim, float a boat, fish or just sit and watch while feeding the ducks. I loved to skip stones across the water and spent many hours pursuing this activity. At night, lake dwellers were treated to a chorus of frogs and insects welcoming the stars and moon to the sky with their music. Bogie Lake was an upper class Huck Finn paradise.

While the house on the lake was being built I used to crawl around underneath it in all the dark places. I had a great love for dark places as a child. I would be scared and excited at the same time. The danger of not knowing what was ahead made my heart thump loudly in my chest. I would cautiously crawl forward into the darkness, my head spinning with fantasies. I can still smell the damp air, feel the powdery dust and hear the sounds of the contractors working on the house above me. Every deep shadow hid monsters waiting to spring out, snatch me with their sharp claws dripping with the blood of their last victim and drag me off to an even darker lair where I most assuredly would be devoured. My skin would crawl, and the hair on the back of my neck would stand up when, finally something only half seen and very gruesome would fling itself at me. I would spin around, sometimes bumping my head on a support beam, and scramble through the dust to emerge wide-eyed with my heart bursting from my

chest and a tingling in my toes. The monster had
nearly gotten me! If only adults could find plea-
sures so simple.   Around 1960, the family saw
some hard economic times, resulting in bankruptcy.
This was to bring about a few changes that would
make life a little better for me. Our primary place of
residence became the house on Bogie lake. I had always loved the lake and the house on it. There were
many good times associated with Bogie Lake. Probably the best part of it was that John was not there
much of the time. He was in California staying with
a friend while he sought work. The periods of his
absence were truly wonderful.

We lived at the lake for about two years. During this time some important changes took place. The
first change was that John got out of the habit of
beating on me all the time, though the urge never
quite left him and still had to be satisfied once in
awhile. I still had to endure his violence at times. In
addition, I was to observe Doris' transmutation from
Queen of the Ball to cleaning lady. We no longer had
the money to afford a maid or handyman, and with
John in California much of the time, it was Doris
who had to keep the household going. That included
the cooking, cleaning and whatever else had to be
done to keep the household in order. If that wasn't
enough, Doris was reduced to cleaning other people's
houses so we could have enough money to live on.

The fall from Queen to char lady must have hurt her in ways only she could know. She was never as violent as John was and, with all she had to do, her attention was turned away from me. Her unhappiness with her new station and her constant battle to cope with life in the trenches gave me a break.

The instrument of the family bankruptcy seems to have been a certain business deal inspired by a man who owed John some money. The man tendered John an offer of two dollars worth of stock for each dollar he owed, in effect, making John a general partner of the man's manufacturing firm located in Florida. As the story goes, the man embezzled the company assets. John was left holding the bag. He not only lost all the money owed to him, but because he entered into a general partnership with this man, he was liable for all of the bills owed by the company. Instead of doubling his take, John doubled his loss.

The man who sold John the interest in the company can be heaped with his share of the blame. He might have had the idea of embezzlement in mind when the transaction took place. But the real downfall of the family finances was greed.

With the roof caving in on the family, I was able to actually begin enjoying my childhood. I was still beaten occasionally and told that I was a lame brain or, in Doris' favorite terminology, "a little bas-

tard." John would flit back to the roost in Michigan
every so often and stay long enough for Doris to have
stories to tell him about the miserable little bastard I
had been. The customary whipping would follow.

On one of his trips back to Michigan near the
beginning of this period, John became exceedingly
violent. I can remember the incident but not the reason. I was suddenly seized, dragged from my chair
and shoved into the bathroom. Something very much
like a speeding locomotive whizzed from behind me
and smashed into the side of my face about the time
I turned to look.

When I came to, I found myself crumpled on
the floor with a galaxy of stars orbiting my head.
Blood bubbled out of my mouth from a large gash
on the inside of my cheek. My jaw was broken, and
I was experiencing that feeling of weakness and unre-
ality one has when the body is in shock. As my head
cleared, it came to me that I needed a doctor.

Several family members were by then standing in the bathroom or near the door. They were
rooted to the spot like trees in the park. No one
seemed to be moving toward the phone to call the
doctor. They were all just standing and staring at me
like people morbidly fascinated with a terrible traffic accident. I received no medical attention other
than some hot water with Epsom salts. I did not understand, then, why they didn't take me to the doc-

tor. I understand now. How could they have explained my broken jaw to the doctor or the police?

From that moment on I have had a constant clicking sound in my jaw each time I bite down. The noise was forgotten for a few years because my molars had abscessed due to the effects of alcoholism. It is very difficult to care for one's teeth when one is passed out day in and day out, year after year, from drinking a quart of whiskey a day. Recently, I was equipped with complete dentures, so now I have molars again and the constant clicking to remind me of that day.

The reader might wonder why I have included this incident in a chapter entitled "The Good Times." The main reason is this, even in the good times, there were unspeakable atrocities committed upon my small body and mind. At the time of this incident I was about ten and certainly did not deserve this kind of punishment from an adult no matter what the crime. The other reason is that my jaw was broken at the beginning of the family crisis. It marked a turning point in my relations with John and Doris. I was still beaten once in awhile, but never this severely again. Perhaps somewhere in their minds they recognized that John had been out of control. After having thought about the consequences of being discovered in their abuse, they may have developed a healthy fear, healthy for me as well, of what could happen should the police find out. None of this line of thought was ever communicated to me. Nothing of importance ever was. I was just some dumb kid who couldn't understand anyway. Why try to communicate anything more complicated than two or three word commands that ended in my nickname, Little Bastard?

Some of the time I did do pretty dumb things, just like a lot of other children do in their growing up. For instance, many times I was sent to bed without dinner, as a punishment, and then told not to get into the refrigerator. Tell a fish not to swim. It's easier. I became very sneaky at stealing food from the refrigerator. I learned that it did not pay to take a lot of one thing because it would be missed, and then I'd be in hot water. I took a little of everything so it would not be noticed. I also learned to eat fast. I had a fear that if I did not finish my food quickly, John or Doris would take it away and send me to my room. I still inhale my food as if there will be no more tomorrow.

One day, while we were staying at the house on the lake, Doris went off somewhere with the final admonition that I stay away from the refrigerator. I watched her leave, just to be sure. After she had been gone for a few minutes, I went to work. A little piece of this bread, a spoonful of noodles, a crumb of cheese and a splat of mashed potatoes. As I loaded the last bite into my mouth, the noise of Doris returning startled me. I hurriedly closed the refrigerator door and slid into another room. Doris went straight to the kitchen and the refrigerator. I was feeling elated at having gotten away so cleanly when I heard the refrigerator door slam and footsteps approaching. It was too late to hide. Suddenly, I found myself towed by the ear to the kitchen. Doris asked me if I had been in the refrigerator. I felt confident that my tracks had been well covered, so I lied. She swung the door open, and I was confronted with my frosty eyeglasses sitting on the top shelf next to the milk. When John returned home, I received a hot seat for this incident. The story is humorous now, but I couldn't smile then. I relate this not because of the spanking I received, but because of the lie I told. By this time, lying was firmly planted in my personality. Call it a survival instinct, if you will, for that is just what it was. I eventually became a pathological liar and spent half a lifetime overcoming this dysfunction.

Nevertheless, life at Bogie Lake was much better. I loved climbing trees of which there was an abundance. I sought the same thrill that I sought while under the house, only there was a more immediate danger to my activities. That is why they were forbidden. But could I let that stop me? Not when my astrological sign is Leo.

The best tree climbing days were when the

wind was blowing. I used to climb as close to the top
as I could get and hang on for dear life as the tree
swayed in the wind. Life is seen in a different light
from fifty or a hundred feet in the air. The adrenaline
gets to flowing, and you can't help but wonder what
would happen if a sudden gust of wind. . . Scary!
As I've said before, I liked to be scared when I was
young.

Winter at the lake was fabulous. Michigan has
more than its share of snow and cold freezing weather
that solidifies the top layer of the state's lakes. Sometimes a bunch of us kids would get together and
shovel the snow off the lake to make a skating rink.
A tough job at the least. Occasionally, when the conditions were ideal, some of the fathers would use
their jeeps with snowplows on the front to do in a
matter of minutes what it would take hours for kid-
labor to do.

When the snow was cleared, it was time for
hockey. That little black puck was to me what a pill
is to a junkie. Nothing else mattered when I was on
the ice. A semi truck could have fallen out of the sky
and landed next to me, and I wouldn't have noticed
as long as I didn't fall into the hole it made. While
playing, I would forget my troubles and take out my
frustrations in the play. When we were through, I
felt invigorated and could not help but look around
at the snow-covered beauty around me. That cold

snow, sparking like diamonds, and contrasting with
the dark green of the trees, is enough to take anyone's
breath away. It even helped to dull the pains I felt
from overextending muscles, banging down hard on
the ice, or engaging in a fight when the game heated
up.

Kathy loved to skate, too. She didn't play
hockey. That was strictly for us boys. But she could
skate rings around me and did so every chance she
had.. She displayed the grace and beauty of a balle-
rina on ice skates. She was perky, quick, and so full
of happiness and impishness. Kathy used to taunt
me to catch her. I would chase her all over the ice,
but the effort always ended in failure.

When we were finished skating and came in
from the cold, stiff and sore, with faces rubbed red
by the wind, each one of us would be made to drink
this concoction of John's. I would hold my breath
and gulp it down, so I wouldn't have to taste it. In a
few minutes the physical sensations of light-
headedness and loss of motor control would begin.
The effect was incredibly satisfying. A warm and
almost magical transformation took place in my body
and my mind. The concoction was a mixture of
brandy and herbs, probably an old Lithuanian remedy.

Life at Bogie lake was one of the bright spots
in my existence. It will always be treasured along

with those other times when life seemed good and worth living. I can assure you that I am a much happier person now than I have ever been. Whenever I am down I relive one of the happier episodes in my life. It keeps me from feeling the pain again, and from feeling sorry for myself for having to remember all the muck that made parts of my life hell.

CHAPTER FOUR
California Here I Come

We were just "dumb" kids, but we knew something was up. John and Doris weren't telling us something. John was home, and had been home for longer than usual. There were several visitors who came during this period, some to talk behind closed doors with John alone, others talked with both John and Doris. We didn't pay attention at first, but when John didn't leave for California and people kept coming and the phone kept ringing, I began to sneak around to see what was happening.

At about the same time, John and Doris told us we were going to Pennsylvania to live. That is when everything suddenly became an upheaval. Packing was done, fast and furious. Before we all knew it, everything was ready. All of us piled into a new Cadillac, and as we pulled out of the driveway, John told us we were actually going to California. We immediately interpreted it to mean Disneyland. All of us kids were ecstatic. We couldn't understand this last minute change of plans, but it mattered little. The only thing that mattered, besides going to Disneyland, was that we hadn't been able to gloat to our friends about such an adventure. We had told every one we were going to Pennsylvania. That was just what Doris and John had wanted.

The bill collectors from the failed business in Florida had been hot and heavy on John's tail. He had counted on us to spread the news that we were moving to Pennsylvania to misdirect them. For years after we moved, John's nephew, whose name is also John Bubnes, received phone calls and visitors trying to collect on the bad debts my adopted father left behind. I found this out in 1982, when I called John's nephew from my place in California.

We were able to move in a brand new Cadillac because John's new business was selling cars. His boss owned the car that had to be moved to California so it could be delivered to a waiting customer.

We lived in Pacoima, California, for a couple of months before moving to Northridge. I turned thirteen in Northridge. It was here that Doris caught me masturbating. I remember peering through my thick glasses and being told that I would go blind if I kept on masturbating. I trembled to think of it.

John and Doris sent me to a shrink. They gave me the label "little pervert." I was certain I was going to go blind. When they found out I was sweet on a girl, they accused me of molesting her. She emphatically told her parents that I had not touched her. The truth was believed by her parents, yet my parents still thought I had done it, and treated me with an underlying disgust, much as how one would react when they turn back the bed- covers and find a pile of vomit.

Before school started, we moved to Modesto, California. I attended Our Lady of Fatima where I became an altar boy and sang in the choir. I went on to Grace Davis High School where I began my drinking career. I was kicked out of several dances and clearly had a developing problem, but my behavior was quietly tolerated. The school took no action against me. People who were responsible for dealing with me didn't, so I didn't deal with the problem either. The result, of course, was that the dimensions of my aberrant behavior loomed larger with each passing year.

In order to please John and Doris, I went out for freshman football. I tried out for several positions and wound up as a starting lineman. Sports for me were nothing to be fanatical about, but it was a way of gaining attention. I had hoped that my adopted parents would take notice if I did something positive. We had a winning team. We won two championships. John and Doris never came to my games. They preferred to stay home and sip highballs instead. I played on the Varsity Squad and during one important game was appointed captain by the coach. Just before the last game, however, I was caught smoking and as a result didn't play in the final game.

Dan Gonsalves, Varsity Football Coach, whom I have stayed in touch with over the years, was asked what he remembered about me in those high school years. Here is his reply:

"My first direct personal contact with Brian Bubnes was when he joined the Varsity Football Team at Grace M. Davis High School in the fall of 1965. I had observed this hyperactive young man when he was with the Sophomore squad the previous year, and had wondered then whether he would mature enough to be able to make the transition to the more demanding and competitive varsity level.

Brian was indeed a challenge. He was a free-spirited young man. He was easy to please, but his focus was fluid.

He loved to talk. What he said wasn't always accepted by his teammates and/or the coaching staff in the manner he had hoped. "He was a little off the wall," as we say in the 90's.

But, he had courage and this virtue is what got him through his junior year.... a year of adjustment for Brian.... a year of paying his dues physically and mentally and getting very little playing time.

The off season between his jun-

ior/senior year was one filled with ups and downs, near misses with eligibility, discipline confrontations, training rule problems, but he always landed on his feet. Keeping his seemingly upbeat attitude, he moved forward.

By his senior year, Brian had matured physically and fought his way into a starting position as an offensive guard on our football team. He was quick and strong. He developed into one of our best offensive linemen. His main problem was still not controlling his remarks so as not to alienate team members. From time to time players and coaches alike did wonder about Brian, as the popular teen saying went, being "goofy."

I personally liked Brian's "freshness" or "free spirit." It did give us a little variety on our team and, believe it or not, it alleviated the sometimes tedious practice time. He did stretch my patience to the limit on occasion. This inconsistency of Brian's actions did reach a climax when I had to discipline him for breaking training rules and smoking. I suspended him from our fi-

nal game of the season.

The most pleasing memory of Brian during that senior year was when I appointed him co-captain for our crucial game against our inter-city rival, Modesto High School. Twenty-five years later I can still see his beaming smile when I told him he was captain. His expression was one of great pride and total commitment to the task. He was so happy, so pleased. Over the many years that I have had the opportunity to give young athletes the responsibility of leadership, few have reacted with the degree of unmasked feelings that Brian exhibited that day. I will always remember that moment. Knowing what I now know about Brian's back-
ground, I suspect that some of his reactions can be attributed to his deep desire for acceptance. Regardless of the reason, I'm glad that Brian got his chance to lead his peers.

Since his high school years our paths have crossed numerous times. It is always interesting to talk with Brian about his latest experiences, whether

*they are professional or personal in
nature. Most recently, he has worked as
a substitute teacher in our schools, and
yes, he has been a substitute for me.
We've come full circle, one might say.
Brian does have real potential as a
teacher.*

*Brian is an interesting young
man. He has traveled a difficult road.
He came a long way. He deserves a little
sunshine in his life."*

I tried out for basketball, but when I kept getting hit in the back of the head due to my inattention,
I was cut from the squad.

In the summer of 1965, an event that was to
change my life occurred: Kathy left home never to
return. I remember being in bed that night and opening my eyes to see John, Doris, Kathy and my adopted
brother, Jon, all standing in the hallway. They were
visible through the door that was left ajar. It was evident that they were having a serious discussion. I
was unable to determine what was said because the
door swung shut. The next morning, Kathy was gone.
No one would tell me anything. I had no clue as to
what had happened. The Academy Awards were
given to the wrong people that year.

I didn't learn anything about this until 1981,

after John died. A few days before he died, I went to
see him at Celeste Manor. He had suffered several
strokes, yet physically he looked fine. They brought
him out in a wheel chair. It became clear his mind
was gone. All he said was, "Take it off, baby," over
and over.

While the old man was lying in state for viewing, my sister bent over the open casket and put her
face right next to his and stayed there for about a
half-hour. I believe Kathy got very drunk a few days
after the funeral. I had no idea what was coming.
She was letting out a lot of pent up feelings that
needed release, and I was the one chosen to listen.
John had done something to her repeatedly while
Doris attended night school at Modesto Junior College. She had gone to Doris about it. Doris gave her
no protection. Doris continued her night school which
gave John the opportunity to do it again and again.
Doris did give her some advice, "Wear five more
pair of underwear."

I believe that Kathy was still protecting me. If
I had known what John did to her, I would probably
have gone to prison for killing him.

After Kathy left, life changed. The home
seemed mellower than it had been. I was not subject
to physical abuse again, though the threat of it still
remained, and the mental abuse continued. I was still
a dumb perverted little bastard. I was also still kept

in the dark as to family matters, especially anything having to do with my sister moving out. Much of my time was spent either at school or away from the house. When I couldn't take it any more, I would run away for a few days. This always caused some conflict, but John and Doris seemed to have lost the old fire and fell to fighting more among themselves than with me.

One activity that kept me out of the house was doing yard work. One of my best customers was a Mrs. Irene Bonner. She was an eccentric old lady who lived alone, except for her two Chihuahuas, in a large house with a large yard, and a Steinway piano in the living room. She drank whiskey and smoked too much, but was very kind and often offered me iced lemonade while I was working. One day, while sweating in the hot Valley sun, she heard me singing as she brought me a cold drink. "What a lovely voice you have!" she exclaimed. "Would you like me to be your voice coach?" I was taken back by this compliment combined with an offer that seemed bogus to me at the time. I had learned to mistrust adults. They always had ulterior motives that had to do with their gain and my loss. "No," I said suspiciously. I later learned that Irene Bonner was an internationally famous singer, the world's number one diva, when she was younger. She sang the lead in Pucini's La Boheme. She sang at the New York Metropolitan

Theater and all over the world. With her coaching and connections, I could have made a career in singing were it not for the mistrust I had developed for adults. Three years ago she died and left the Steinway to Modesto Junior College along with several original manuscripts written by great composers.

Another occupation that kept me out of the house was getting in trouble. I encountered the forces of the law several times while in high school. In one instance, I was parked out in the country with my date. We had a six-pack of beer in the car when a sheriff's officer investigated us.

On another occasion, a bunch of us decided to go party at Woodward Reservoir one weekend. We put all of our party gear on inner tubes and air mattresses and swam out to an island thinking that the park rangers would leave us alone out there, because it would be too much trouble to come get us. Instead, they just got in their boat and came out. When they got there to investigate, all our beer was in my ice chest. One officer asked us whose ice chest it was. Not realizing the trouble I would be in, I claimed ownership and was immediately arrested. I was the only one prosecuted. It is lucky that I was already signed up to enter the Air Force. The judge told me clearly that it was time for me to either go to jail or get into the service to straighten my life out. I wonder how many others were straightened out by the

67   Tennesee Tears

military.

Responsibility was one load that was never put on my shoulders. As a result, I didn't learn responsibility for my actions until many years into adulthood. The one responsibility that I wanted the most to shoulder was that of driving a car. This was denied me. As a result, I had to attach myself to other guys who had cars and were willing to take me places. This was done in exchange for my finding for them what they were unable to find for themselves—dates. This turned out to be an equitable arrangement.

I seldom saw my sister during this time. The exception was school. She continued to attend, and I would see her in the course of the day. Whenever I found out where she was outside of school, I would go see her. I must admit that I had reasons for seeing her that had nothing to do with brotherly love, although I did then and still do love my sister dearly. Kathy hung out with older boy friends that had access to alcohol. Seeing her usually meant getting drunk as well. She also developed a taste for alcohol, which she has to this day. Like me, her drinking has taken her over the boundaries of excess. There was one thing she never did, she never went home again.

Since 1965, my sister has made only a few attempts to stay in touch with me. Whenever we have been in touch, it has usually been because I wanted to hear from her. She has always wanted children, yet has had very little contact with her niece and nephew. All of her energy has been concentrated in finding a man. Each one she meets is the one for her and each relationship fails. Sis has been married five times. It is uncanny how all of the men she has attached herself to, have, in my opinion, been psychologically similar to our adopted father, John.

CHAPTER FIVE
Running Away

There is a trait among alcoholics that is called "geographicalism". This refers to the alcoholic's propensity to evacuate to another location to start a new life. The new life fails, of course, because the alcoholic only succeeds in bringing the old problems into a new setting. Most people will recognize this as an elaborate form of running away.

I began running away from home at about the time we moved to Modesto. I used to stay away for three days at a time. There was one time when Doris spotted me in the alley behind our house. I was elated. There she was, not more than fifty feet from me crying and begging me to stay. "Things will change. You'll see. It will be better," she pleaded. But I discovered in that moment that I had power over my life. I knew I could outrun her if I wanted to. Her pleading made her look so pathetic. "Please, Brian, please come home." Her tears dripped down her cheeks spattering on the dirt in the alley.

"Right," I told myself, "She just wants me to get close enough so she can grab me and beat the hell out of me." I had been through this scene before. I also knew from past experience that our family was beyond change. Doris and John were never going to stop drinking and fighting. They would always think of me as the stupid little bastard. John and Doris couldn't help themselves. I wouldn't allow myself to trust them under any circumstances, and I certainly wasn't going to fall for a trick already played on me before.

Eventually, I did return, and life at home mellowed out for awhile. Doris and I actually began to get along together. Doris, our neighbor, and I would spend peaceful days getting drunk at the house. Alcohol again removed the reality from life for me. It doesn't get any worse than this.

When I ran away, it was not very far, and John and Doris usually knew where I was. I would go over to a friend's house to stay. There were two friends and their parents, the Lucas family and the Johnson family, who made this possible. When I arrived and it was certain that I was going to stay, the parents would phone up John and Doris to let them know where I was. I was always made to feel welcome at these homes.

One time I ran away to San Francisco. I remember walking along the wharf, through Northbeach and exploring the city streets and parks. Other times I went out to get soused with my drinking buddies. I was picked up for vagrancy once. I remember John coming down to get me. On the way home, driving up McHenry Avenue, he asked me if I was ready to straighten up and go home or did I want to go to Juvenile Hall? Without batting an eyelid, I told him, "Take me to Juvenile Hall." My wishes went unfulfilled.

My hatred for John built up over the years. After all, the man was big, and he used that size advantage to force me to his will. He terrorized me. He gave me no respect, yet demanded it for himself. Great fantasies hurled around in my head. I could see myself pounding the crap out of him with blood flowing everywhere. He would cry for mercy, and I would give none. I wanted to kill him. When I ran away, I was not only running away from being bludgeoned and mentally abused in my own home, I was running away from my raging anger.

Then there was the time I came home at one o'clock in the morning. I thought that John and Doris would already be in bed, but found John sitting at the kitchen table drinking a highball and Doris cutting up some food at the counter, between sips of her drink. The minute he saw me, John started in. "Where have you been, you little bastard?" he shouted. He ejected from his chair and flew at me. All that hatred and anger came to the surface of my mind. There was fear there as well. I knew what would happen if he got hold of me. Before I knew it, I had laid him on the ground with a single blow. I honestly don't know who was more surprised, I or John. Without that surprise, I am certain that I would never have been able to knock him down. He was still much larger than I and would have pulverized me had he known I was going to swing at him.

John started to get up. He was very hot, and his face was as red as a fire engine. The surprise quickly melted into a megaton of anger. Doris, still clutching the large butcher knife she had been using, pushed between us and started shouting. She waved the knife around while she shouted.

So here I was, scared out of my wits, with this woman gone crazy waving the big knife around and shouting, and there was John struggling to get up so he could smash my face in. I did the only sensible thing that could be done, I left for three days. There was a paper drive going on at Our Lady of Fatima, and I went to sleep in the paper bin. The paper bin wasn't exactly a home away from home, so I spent the last part of this time at the Lucas home.

I ran away from my problems, by running away from home, where I encountered more problems with the law. Then I joined the Air Force and caused more problems to run away from. Out of the service, I moved frequently. I was still running away. Ultimately, running away led me deeper into a bottle that was supposed to take me away from all my problems. Most alcoholics feel their poison helps by anesthetizing them and erasing the painful episodes from their lives. It doesn't. It seems to work for awhile, but when a certain level of intoxication is reached, the dragon rears its ugly head, and the host becomes fixated on what they were trying to forget. The bottom line is that the pain continues to affect the life of the chronic alcoholic. Ask any person who has been involved with a drinker who is running away. They will tell you. And if you listen closely, you will hear how they were affected as well.

Of course, when one runs into the bottle and keeps running deeper and deeper into its recesses, there comes the day when they smash against the bottom and cannot go any further. Then there is only one way out which does not require detox—DEATH.

My second wife, Nancy Ryan, had just left me because she couldn't handle my drinking, God bless her. She did it for herself, because she couldn't make a difference in my life. I went through a three-day detoxification program and came home to what had been our house. All of her stuff had been packed up and taken away. The house seemed empty without her and her things there. It was still a mess both from her hasty exodus and the ripping and tearing I had done while I was drunk. I cleaned up everything. I even threw away all the alcohol in the house. I had gone three days without a drink and felt I didn't need one.

I wanted Nancy back. I thought that if I quit drinking, I would get her back. There was not a more

determined drunk in the world at the time, determined
to quit, that is. The house looked so pretty when I
had finished that I began thinking about getting just
one bottle of wine to sort of celebrate my newfound
resolve and my new life with Nancy. I got the wine,
drank it and somehow wound up with more than I
had bargained for. It wasn't long before yours truly
was sloppy. At one point I called up my brother down
in Escalon, and told him I needed help, could he
please come and get me? He and his wife arrived
and took me home with them. I spent a sober day at
his place, but his wife was very uneasy with me there
in the condition I was in. A hangover isn't very pretty
when it is from several years of continual drinking.

I went home, got drunk and laid on my
waterbed spitting at the walls, because I was "grown
up" and could do it. I ran up a tremendous phone bill
calling talk show hosts and other people on long distance lines. I called up a couple of the local ministers. To my surprise they came over to talk to me.
They tried to get me to go with them so they could
help me. When the ministers left, I began to have
thoughts of shooting myself. I stared at myself in the
mirror with the gun ready to blow my head off my
shoulders. I suddenly realized that this was stupid. I
couldn't let my life end like this, not if I could help
it. Ultimately, what stopped me was the last vestige
of hope that remained, hope I would find my real

family someday.

For anyone who would like to run away from his or her troubles, I would say that running away is a gas that blows up in your face.

CHAPTER SIX
Doing the Backstroke In A Bottle

While hockey was my physical outlet when I was a boy, the folk remedy of my adoptive parents was to be embraced later in my life as an outlet for emotions I couldn't deal with and a cure for all that ails. Believe me, I ailed plenty. The Lithuanian remedy took away the pains accumulated while playing hockey, and the alcohol I drank later took away the pains accumulated over a lifetime, or so I thought. Most alcoholics believe that their bottle helps them forget. It really doesn't. The pain just seems to be more bearable for a time. The real kicker is that when one is ready to face it, years of drinking actually intensify the hurt. Every one has hurdles to jump in life, but an alcoholic, though they might run the same track, sets their hurdles higher than everyone else does. Failure becomes a form of success.

My excuse began with a sleep disorder probably caused by the beatings I took at bedtime. The awful stuff I had to drink after hockey games did make me relax, and I noticed how easily I was able to sleep on nights when this potion was administered. Even a mental midget is able to discern what feels good and sort out what works from what does not. It didn't take long for me to realize that pain avoidance was inside a bottle in the liquor cabinet.

At about the age of fourteen I began stealing my adopted father's vodka. The theft of the contraband was covered up by replacing that which was taken with a common clear liquid we all know and use—water. I would hate to try to estimate the number of alcoholics who have used this clever and efficient method of obtaining their heart's desire.

Alcohol was not just available in my home. It was also available at the home next door. Our neighbors drank a great deal of beer. A can or two from the refrigerator was never missed. A healthy chug from a bottle while its owner was busy in the bathroom was low risk as well. There was a local wino that used to buy us booze in high school in exchange for money to purchase his beer. He would stagger into the liquor store and get what we wanted along with a six-pack for himself. It was amazing. He was so wasted that in the time it took him to enter the store, he forgot what we wanted. You can be sure he remembered what he wanted. We sometimes laughed at his inability to keep it together, that is, when we weren't irritated at not being served our favorite poison. The irony was that it would not be very long before I would become the object I laughed at as a young drinker. The time when I began to have blackouts was just around the corner.

One of my memories is throwing up on my bedroom floor at the tender age of seventeen. Barbecue potato chips and cherry vodka were the culprits. You can decide which one contributed the most. My head was spinning, and my system desperately needed to rid itself of the unaccustomed high level of poison.

I got kicked out of my share of dances for being too drunk to maintain. During the summer after graduation from high school, I drank a lot of beer. I would suffer from slight headaches, nothing serious. It was easy to go out working and sweat it out. A young body has a high tolerance for abuse.

After summer was over, I joined the Air Force. I barely got in as a Category 4. Eleven years later I retook the test and scored in Category 1.

I have often tried to remember the bus ride to my first assignment. All that comes to me is that I took the ride with a soldier from West Point Military Academy, New York, and named Brown. Brown had a bottle of Seagram's Seven that we drank with lemonade. We raised a commotion on the bus that apparently disturbed every one but us. We kept reaching up to pull the emergency cord because we had to go to the bathroom. The bus driver became very angry. I'm surprised he didn't toss us out the window without slowing down. I remember pulling into the gate at the base and some exchange of clothes or bedding. I must have passed out then, because the next thing I remember I awoke and found all my clothes nicely hung up and the odor of mothballs contributing to a terrible hangover.

I was lonely in the service and my loneliness greatly contributed to the drinking problem. A lot of drinking went on in the barracks. It seemed like every one drank. I stayed drunk as much as possible, even to the point of passing out in snow banks. I was always stumbling into trouble.

The problem was intensified from the moment I realized that alcohol made me feel better, and it was a waste to use it on sleep alone. Why not drink all the time, so I could feel good all the time? I would drink anything and wake up in the morning, throw up and begin it all over again. Blackouts added to the other perceived enhancements alcohol was providing because they gave me less of my life to think about. Unfortunately, I learned just enough about what I did during these episodes to be scared. There is nothing like waking up the next morning and not knowing where you parked your car the night before or even how you got home. Once I threw six people into a swimming pool in a fit of drunkenness and did not know of it until a couple of people told me when I sobered up. The worst part was not being sure of what I had done or said. I couldn't trust authority, I couldn't trust other people, and the bottom line was that I couldn't trust myself.

I can kid about this now, but I assure you that

underneath the kidding there is a part of me that realizes the seriousness of what I went through. I used to keep my alcohol in my car. I had no need to hide my booze; I hadn't promised anyone I would stop drinking. There was a feeling of control, as I had the only key to the car. This probably contributed to the drunk driving ticket I received in 1978. I am very lucky not to have injured or killed anyone.

It was also a damn miracle that I got through college. I was able to do this because I kept pushing my body and my mind. Added to this was the intense hatred I felt for my family. The majority opinion was that I was too stupid to be a Bubnes. It was not that the Bubnes family was all well educated. Aunt Albina, John's sister, was the only Bubnes to hold a degree. They were just arrogant. I decided at a very young age that I would earn my degree, and if any of the family opened their mouths, I would stuff my degree down their throats.

I worked my way through college, sometimes working two part time jobs. I also received money from the GI Bill for Education. I arranged my schedule so that my classes were all on Tuesday and Thursday. This freed up Mondays, Wednesdays and Fridays for my work which included working as a shipping clerk for a wholesale grocery and even officiating at local high school sporting events. I even had time to work for the Air Force Reserves.

My high school grades weren't very good, so I began junior college where I earned a "C" average. I went on to regular college at California State College Sonoma where I earned a degree in business despite being on academic probation from the start. Later, I was to begin work on a Master's in Special Education that I haven't finished yet. I would have worked myself to death to get that piece of paper, if that's what it took. I wanted so much to wave that degree in the faces of my family that death seemed a reasonable alternative. Yet I found the time to drink.

I used to love to drink seven up and brandy when I arrived home from work. My first wife and I split up when I reached the point where I was drinking a quart of brandy a day. I just told her that I couldn't stay with her straight, and I couldn't stay with her loaded. That's when I got the courage to break up with her.

In 1979 I went through my first detox. By then I had broken up with my second wife. I went to detox for the wrong reason. I did it for her. I wanted her back in my life. I bounced back and forth attending two different detox centers. One of them was an alcoholic rehab institution.

When I finally decided it was time to be sober, I did it primarily on my own, because I wanted to, because I couldn't stand life or myself any more while drunk. I began attending AA meetings for support. I had attended them off and on since 1979, with no effect, but this time was different. I had decided it was time to be sober. By this time all of my old associates were gone, and new people were entering my life. AA gave me the support I needed to keep on the sober track.

Things eventually got better for me. I am extremely scared of alcohol now, yet I tease myself. I have these fantasies. Some guys fantasize about Farah Fawcett. I fantasize about a drink. Every fiber of my being knows I cannot have it. Sometimes I say that was years ago. "Man, you can handle it. Your emotional life is all squared away. Go for it." I laugh at this, because I know I can't lie to myself.

CHAPTER SEVEN
The Search

In January, 1971, I was a freshman at Santa Rosa Junior College in Santa Rosa, California. My first child, Jennifer, had been born in 1969 at West Point Military Academy. The pregnancy was an unplanned one. Her mother, who was about eight years my senior, had wanted an abortion and had made arrangements to go to Georgia for this purpose. I talked her out of it, we married, and Jennifer was born.

I had continued to harbor the hope that I would some day find my biological family, but now I had another reason—Jennifer. I assumed it would at some time be important to her, as it had been to me all those years, to have knowledge of her roots and to be acquainted with members of her true family. I had a great plan. I would find them and then they and I would just hug each other for the rest of eternity. And John and Doris? I would simply forget them and go on with the business of living after I had told my real parents of the cruelties I had endured at the hands of John and Doris: The next order of business would be to tell my parents I love them and introduce them to my child and my wife. Following that, I would observe the happiness of my sister as she discovered the family she thought lost forever. I would ask them what had gone wrong. Why did they have to put Sis and me up for adoption? Next, I would etch their faces in my mind so I would never lose them again and then I would feel loved and never be lonely again. End of story. Lights fade out on a small knot of people hugging each other and crying tears of happiness.

With this scenario in mind, I mailed a request for copies of my adoption records to St. Peter's Orphanage in Memphis, Tennessee. Weeks passed as I tried to find things to occupy my mind, so I wouldn't be thinking about the expected arrival of my life and thus making the time seem much longer than it was. Finally, the reply arrived. I was crushed. The notice informed me that all adoption records had been shipped to Nashville, Tennessee and were sealed permanently. We need a disclosure law to prevent this from happening again.

My expectations had gotten so high that when they were not met, I went into depression. There is no other experience in this life like having the jaws of the great abyss open up beneath your feet and suck you down into that pain filled cavern. Then there is the anger you feel at being singled out for this unique experience coupled with self pity that makes you forget that there are other people in this world who have had it a lot worse than you.

In desperation, I again asked Doris for more information on my biological family. She said there was none. Instead of assisting me in my hour of need, she helped to quash my hopes. Sometime later, I was to receive a rumor via Doris that my mother had gone back to the orphanage and stolen me. According to the story, she then ran off to Chicago where she was apprehended by the law. What was her purpose in spreading this story?

The depression passed. It would hit me again and again over the years, but each time hope would pull me through. After seven years of marriage, we split up. My next wife was the baby-sitter. She didn't get pregnant, but I did manage to drink the marriage away.

My third wife came along a couple of years later. We were living together, and she stopped taking her birth control pills without telling me. The result was Andrew, born in May of 1982. I married her to make Andrew legitimate. I didn't want a child of mine to be labeled a bastard. The marriage lasted nine months. When I asked her why she had quit taking the birth control pills, I was informed that they were making her sick and she was afraid I would get angry.

Shortly after Andrew was born, I received notification that I was to attend a three-week Army National Guard Administrators' School at Camp Richardson near Little Rock, Arkansas. Though I hated tearing myself away from my infant son, the army's call had to be answered. Besides, the school would benefit me both personally and professionally. I also quickly realized that Little Rock is only one hundred fifty miles from Memphis, Tennessee. There was a shred of hope that I would be able to go there and find some piece of the puzzle I had nearly given up hope of ever solving. My brain went into overdrive to try to figure out a way to travel from Little Rock to Memphis. Fantasy after fantasy tantalized my mind with unfounded hope. The rational part of me realized that I would have to wait until I was at Camp Richardson before I could make any plans, and that even if I got to Memphis, there was the probability I wouldn't find anything to help me. What I didn't realize was that the scene was set, and I was already taken care of.

My first encounter with the humidity that cloaks the Mississippi river basin was distressing. Breathing was difficult. My lungs were used to the arid climate of California. The moisture in the air caused such a deep pain in my chest that I went to the base medical facility in search of relief. I was told that there was no relief, and I would just have to wait a few more days to acclimate my lungs to the humidity.

In the meantime, I gasped and wheezed as I sucked in the water-laden air. Meanwhile, the Arkansas rainstorms came and went. I had never in my

life seen such rain. One minute the sky was clear
and bright, the next minute it would darken with omi-
nous clouds, much like my life. Then the wind would
start whipping up, and in a few minutes the sky would
open, and the rain would pour down. My lungs hurt
so much from the added moisture that I wished for a
set of gills to replace them. The storm would soon
be over and, ghostlike, the clouds would glide away
leaving a wide blue expanse and the knowledge that,
like the episodes of depression in my life, the rain
would return the next day.

Unable to engineer a way of getting to Memphis, my sky filled with dark despair, but before the
storm broke, a ray of sunshine sliced through the
clouds. The base commander, a big handsome man,
told me he was slated to give a commencement
speech at Clemson University. "I'll drive you to the
airport," I volunteered. He looked at me in amaze-
ment as I had taken the words right out of his mouth.

I drove the commander to the airport in Little
Rock. The commander in turn rewarded me with the
use of his late model Cadillac. He placed only one
condition on its use, that I was not to let anyone else
drive his baby. He took off for Clemson, and I left
for Memphis.

Al Cuseuno, a fellow reservist, accompanied
me on the trip. I have since lost contact with Al. This
is my loss as Al was a great companion. I had told

him that I was from St. Peter's Orphanage on Poplar Street in Memphis. I believe Al accompanied me partly out of boredom and partly out of curiosity.

We sped up the long highway to Memphis. The Cadillac was a dream to drive, and our spirits were high, especially mine. The daily thundershower hit, and we cut through it in the lap of luxury. When we reached the Mississippi River, I couldn't believe my eyes. Before me stretched a giant shimmering ribbon crisscrossed with bridges reminding me of the skeletons of prehistoric dinosaurs.

When we arrived in Memphis, I stopped to ask for the location of Poplar Street and St. Peters. The directions were given in the polite Southern style, and we continued on our way. My mind was set on not only seeing where I had been adopted from, but also on gathering any information that might help me find my family. I reasoned that by being there in person, emphasis would be added to show how serious I was about my quest for my biological family. Both doubts and hope filled my thoughts. The doubts began preparing me for a blank wall, and the hopes drove me on towards the inevitable. With my sword unsheathed, I sought the Holy Grail.

For as long as I could remember, recurring images of myself as an infant had flashed through my mind. Sometimes I would be asleep and dreaming when I received these images. Other times I would be totally awake. Then there was the large scar on my leg caused by a serious burn. No one in my life could tell me how it got there, and I couldn't remember. When I thought of going back to the orphanage, even as an adult, fear bubbled to the surface of my mind. I wanted to know what caused this fear. I wanted to know what caused the scar. Most of all, I needed to know what in my memory was fantasy and what was real.

I had never seen pictures of St. Peter's, nor had I ever visited the orphanage since I was adopted at the age of two and a half. When St. Peter's loomed suddenly before me, I felt I was in familiar surroundings. Here were the red brick buildings, there the playground and the black wrought iron fence. The driveway circled the front, just as I had remembered. And the huge oak trees with the squirrels chasing about harvesting the bountiful crop of nuts still existed. The unsettling fear I expected to feel never materialized. It would be years before I would feel it again and solve the mystery of the burn scar. In the meantime, I was in heaven. The most important part was that my floating images had been confirmed in reality. You can't imagine how that felt. If you had been with me, the tears on my cheeks would have been the only testimony of what I was feeling inside.

While there, we met a short, good-looking man

with a warm smile who went by the name of Father Joe. I informed him who I was, and he recalled that I had written him a few years earlier to ask about locating my family. He had only been able to tell me that all of the adoption records had been relocated to Nashville. This statement he repeated to me and added a little tidbit of information that was to keep my hopes from being permanently shattered. He said a movement was afoot to open the adoption records!

As he led us on a tour of the grounds, I became impressed with this gentleman. Kindness and courtesy emanated from his entire being. His understanding was beyond comprehension.

The best part of the tour was when we reached the head of the stairs leading down into the little brick chapel where my sister and I ate our meals. I remembered the child who held his sister's hand. I saw the two small children living in a world so huge, clinging to each other with fear and uncertainty as they carefully descended the stairs. Two tiny children who only had each other. My sister looked out for me then, I recalled, just as she had looked out for me all the years we spent with John and Doris. More tears flowed down my cheeks and splattered on the steps as we descended toward the open door of the chapel and the open door of this chapter of my life.

At this point in time, St. Peter's was no longer the bustling orphanage it had been at the conclusion of W.W.II. There were but a handful of the hundreds of children who had once scampered through the halls and playgrounds. St. Peter's was now geared more toward health care for the elderly. What I didn't know was that in my exploration of St. Peter's, I had passed by my Uncle Tony Scola, my biological mother's brother-in-law. He had been living there in retirement since 1978. I wouldn't learn of this for another decade.

I realize now that my sights were set pretty high. This is a pattern my life has taken on many occasions. A glimmer of hope grows into a bright light that is clouded over by the disappointment of failure. The small successes are obscured.

I bid Father Joe farewell (Years later, Father Joe would be stationed at Camden, Tennessee, the birthplace of my mother) and returned to the car for the drive to Little Rock. The disappointment weighed heavy on my soul, yet I was pleased with myself for having the courage to make the attempt. I didn't consciously realize at the time how much it affected me to know that the visions I had experienced all of my life were based in reality.

On the drive back to Little Rock, I found myself leaving the disappointment behind. After all, there was so much to be thankful for. I had established in my own mind that my recollections of early childhood were based in reality and not fantasy. This was extremely important to my peace of mind as well as my confidence in myself. I had shown courage in going back to the past, and there was the fact that others out there somewhere were working to have the records opened, the records that would reveal the identity of my biological family. Not bad for a day's work.

From 1982 through 1989, I made yearly phone calls to Nashville. Each year my prayers went unanswered, yet I retained enough hope to keep going. Then, in November of 1989, my annual call to Nashville hit pay dirt. Mary Alice Lamb gave me the information I needed to properly request my records. She advised me that there was a tremendous backlog of requests. It would be several months before my efforts would bear fruit. Requests were handled in the order received. I didn't stop to think of the forces at work behind the scenes trying to open those much prized records. All I could think of was that they would soon be mine.

My heart soared like a bird on the wind. Forty years of desolation in the wilderness, and now I was to have a genuine chance to find my family. I was indeed on cloud nine, but underlying all this was the fear of failure, the fear my hopes would be crushed.

I wasted no time in sending out my request for information to the state of Tennessee. Then there was nothing to do but wait. The waiting was not easy.

At times, I would be so full of hope that even the darkest day couldn't discourage me. Then there were the days when the mood shifted into a downswing, and I didn't want to leave my bed. There were other times when I sat at my desk feeling drained of all emotion. Meanwhile, the gears of government in the state of Tennessee seemed to be moving like molasses in January.

To pass the time, I began reading big, thick books. One of those books, "Great Expectations", by Charles Dickens, was about a little orphan boy named Pip. On the morning of June 24, 1990, I finished this book and, still thinking of Pip and Miss Haversham, I went to my post office box to check the mail. There in the box was my first communication from the state of Tennessee.

Ripping open the envelope, I discovered a couple of sheets of paper and a cover letter. The letter read as follows:

> *"Attached is the non-identifying birth family information from your sealed adoption record. A search has been initiated for your birth parents. These services are provided in accordance with your request and the Tennessee Adoption Law.*
>
> *The law authorizes the Depart-*

*ment of Human Services to open the
sealed record in our possession to verify
the identity of the birth parent and to
conduct a search for the parent as verified in the record. The birth parent is the
person who, based upon information contained in the sealed record, has acknowl-
edged that he/she is the parent of the
child.*

> *When the Department locates your
birth parent, we will advise the parent of
your inquiry. With your parent's consent
we will release identifying information
to you. Should your parent not consent
we cannot release identifying information.*

> *We will pursue all leads available
to us in the search for your birth parents. When the search is completed you
will be advised. In the meantime, if you
have questions or concerns feel free to
contact this office."*

The packet included my birth records that in-
dicated that I had been a normal newborn. In addition, there was a physical examination record con-
ducted on December 10, 1951, which explained that
I was a normal two and a half-year-old male child in

excellent physical condition. On both of these records, all of the identifying information was blacked out. My birth name, the names of the hospital and clinic and the doctors who worked on me were all excluded. One page was devoted to non-identifying birth family information. My birth mother was listed as of Scottish descent, Catholic, High School educated, 5'6" tall, about 146 lb., black hair, brown eyes and fair complexion. My birth father was listed as German American, no religion noted, High School educated, 5'7" tall, about 165 lb., black hair, brown eyes and olive skin. Much of this information would later turn out to be incorrect.

The last page was titled, "Health History of Biological Parents and Other Biological Relatives." The information here told me that there are no hereditary diseases or epilepsy on either side of my family. The important part for me was that I had a living grandfather on both sides and two sisters and one brother on Dad's side with another brother and sister on Mom's side of the family. With this many aunts and uncles, there had to be children, cousins of mine who would be my age.

Just a few days after I received this packet of information, Uncle Tony and Cousin Kathleen Scola, relatives from my birth mother's side of the family, received a letter from the State of Tennessee requesting information from them about my mother. A number was included for them to call if they had any information. My cousin and uncle concluded from this that one of my mother's children was searching for the family. They called the number, but the State of Tennessee was unwilling to give them any information. They considered hiring a lawyer to institute a search of their own.

On August 1, 1990, I received another letter from the State of Tennessee. This was to be one of the most important letters I would receive in my life. The letter stated my mother was deceased. It also stated that the State of Tennessee could not locate my birth father. The letter went on to say that since a search had been initiated and completed without finding either of my birth parents alive, I was entitled to send $20 to the Tennessee Department of Health and Environment, Office of Vital Records to receive my original birth certificate.

I was upset that they had said that my mother was dead. I refused to believe it until such time as I could see her grave. On the other hand, though they had not found my dad, they didn't say he was dead. What about his social security number? Did they try to trace him through this little number vital to all Americans?

The more I thought about the situation, the more outraged I became. Here I wanted my family, and all the state of Tennessee could do for me was tell me my mom was dead, and they needed twenty dollars for my birth certificate. What about my mom? Who was she? How did she live? How did she die? What steps had they taken to find Dad? With all I had been through, I figured the State of Tennessee owed me a birth certificate free of charge. I felt a growing anger at the bureaucratic foot dragging that had been going on since I began my search for my birth parents.

"Screw them!" I said to myself, "I won't send them the money."

Feeling that this was not enough, I repeated my statement aloud several times until I was screaming it. My neighbors must have thought I was having a breakdown. I was. I had reason to be having a breakdown. Once again my head had battered the brick wall; Mom was dead, and Dad couldn't be found.

At the time I was opening a restaurant delivery business with a friend of mine, Ira White. I didn't have the time, energy, money or the inclination to deal with these faceless bureaucrats. Looking back on it all, what really brought me down was that I wasn't ready to deal with my mother's death before I had even met her.

Thirteen months later, "Dinner to Your Door," closed down. I went back to substitute teaching and ran into more problems. I got my new dentures and spent that Christmas with Sis and her new boyfriend. I made up my mind that there would be no new disappointments. The future might be uncertain, but what was certain was that I was turning my back on the wall. I cried in my sleep the night I made this decision.

CHAPTER EIGHT
A Friend in Deed

Sometimes in life, we make the acquaintance of someone who becomes so special that the word "friend" does not express the entire meaning of the relationship. In the case of a male/female relationship, outsiders might mistakenly label the two as lovers, but this is only a misconception, and does not express the true depth of feeling between the two people. Karen Johnson has been such a friend to me.

Our two worlds first intersected when we were in high school. Karen was a junior at Grace Davis High School when I was a senior. We had no direct contact with each other while in high school, but there is one image of her I will always remember. It happened when I was due to graduate, a small miracle in itself. I was still not sure they were going to let me graduate. I felt like a cat in a room full of dogs.

The school swimming pool had just been completed, and we had our first opportunity to enjoy the new facility. My love for water, developed during my years at Bogie Lake, brought me to the pool. There was Karen, a beautiful sea nymph, gracefully cutting through the water. Her deep tan showed off the long blonde hair trailing behind her in the pool, and her fine long legs kicked like a dancer's.

At the time, I felt she was too good for me. All

the girls seemed too good for me, but she in particular. We never even spoke to each other during high school. This situation would not be remedied for many years.

In 1980, I had just moved back to Modesto after a thirteen-year absence. I was working as a Modesto City Softball umpire. Sam Dickerson, a rival I had played football against in high school and who later went on to become an All-American wide receiver at the University of Southern California, was my supervisor. This particular evening I was umpiring three women's softball games at Davis Park, adjacent to Davis High School. I was the home plate umpire, and one of the catchers seemed awfully familiar.

At first, I wasn't sure, but after further observation, it turned out to be Karen Johnson. The years had played their games and changed us both. I weighed one hundred and sixty pounds in my senior year. In 1980, I weighed about two hundred twenty pounds and was sporting long hair and a mustache. Karen was more mature looking, but still beautiful.

When I was certain who was doing the catching, I made plans to blow her a kiss the next time she came out of the dugout. It would be interesting to see how she reacted. I didn't think about how anyone seeing the umpire blow the catcher a kiss would have reason to question that umpire's impartiality.

Luckily, no one noticed the kiss blown to Karen except her, and she said nothing aloud, but her look
suggested I was being very rude. I told her who I
was, and the rest is history.

Karen is probably the most disciplined woman
I have ever known. Her family knows full well what
a truly outstanding daughter they have. She is currently a successful elementary teacher and still single
after all these years. It is not because I haven't tried.

Karen's mom, Alice, is almost as close a friend
as Karen is. Being close to me, both of them knew of
my adopted background. It was Alice who mentioned
to Karen that a program about an adoption scandal
was going to be aired on Sunday, January 19, 1992.
Karen not only watched the program, but taped it.
After the taping was done, she called me and asked
if I knew anything about the Tennessee Children's
Home Society in Memphis. When I told her, "No, I
never heard of such a place," she invited me to watch
the tape with her.

So it was that on Monday, January 20, I was
standing on the porch of my friend's home, in the
late afternoon. I was curious about Karen's remarks
to me over the phone. I had spent the entire day
pondering what she meant about the Tennessee Children's Home Society. She gave me few clues about
the program that we were going to watch. Karen
doesn't say much, but when she does, I've learned

to listen. She has my deepest respect. I tried to pry more information out of her, but she wouldn't give the plot away. Karen is a thinker and crafty. She cannot be fooled into divulging information she wishes to keep secret. Her bulldog tenacity, holding on to that information, even teasing me with it, led me to believe that something big was going on. It was my curiosity, and trust in her belief that this was indeed a program I should watch, that brought me to her door.

I knocked and was greeted by the familiar sounds of her two "children," the Davis girls. The Davis "girls" were Baby, a honey colored Cocker Spaniel, and Josephine, an ebony Cocker Spaniel. Baby always fussed over me when I came to visit. So many times I wished it were Karen giving me all those kisses instead of Baby. Josephine, the wilder of the two, bit my nose when I first met her as a pup. Karen got a good laugh out of that.

In I went with the Davis Girls dancing around me in frenzy. My conscience would not allow me to ignore my responsibilities, so I dutifully got down on all fours with the girls for a proper greeting.

Once that ritual was satisfied, I heard Karen say from the kitchen, "We'll have to watch the tape in my bedroom." Her video cassette recorder was located in there. I pretended not to hear her. The Davis Girls and I continued playing.

After a few minutes I looked up at Karen standing in the doorway and said, "You just better behave
yourself." We both knew who'd better behave himself. Just like I knew she would, Karen said, "You
had better behave yourself." "Too late," I said, "I
got you first." I did behave, as acute as the tempta-
tion was.

The four of us piled on the bed and the show
began. After watching the tape, I was exhilarated. I
now knew why Karen had lured me here to watch a
tape of Sixty Minutes. This whole thing happened
around the time and in the same place where I was
born. Was I part of this children's home I had never
heard of? Was I part of this scandalous mess that had
already screwed up the lives of countless people?

During the course of the program I saw much
happiness and much sadness. What I saw renewed
my hope that some day I would find my family. All
of this happened because of two friends who cared.

CHAPTER NINE
Denny Glad

On Friday morning, February 28, 1992, the phone ringing awakened me. I had been anxiously awaiting this phone call for the last several days. The call I was anticipating was to come from Denny Glad, a member of the "Tennessee Right To Know," located in Memphis, Tennessee. This organization was instrumental in persuading the Tennessee State Legislature to change the Tennessee adoption laws. Prior to the change in 1987, all adoption records were totally secret. The change of the law allowed adoptees to request in writing that a search be initiated to find the adoptee's biological parents. If the parents are found, they are advised that their child is searching for them. If either parent rejects the request, the adoptee is blocked from going further.

Denny Glad had been one of the principle people interviewed by Mike Wallace on the Sixty Minutes program Karen had taped for me. She had related that Georgia Tann, the executive secretary of the Tennessee Children's Home Society, in Memphis, and Camille Kelley, Judge of the Juvenile Court, had illegally placed thousands of children during the 1940's. Denny also said that anyone who felt they might need her help could contact her by calling information in Memphis.

Denny has a modest personality. She is diminutive and looks younger than her years. She is as quick as a mongoose, and once she bites into something, she hangs on for dear life. She and her associates have been working on the reform of adoption laws in Tennessee for years. They have not been entirely rewarded by the state legislature. Despite advances in other areas, the secrecy laws that protect the two parties guilty of conceiving a child while locking the innocents away in a dungeon of despair have remained nearly unchanged. An adoptee still requires consent from the biological parents to learn information about themselves.

When I left Karen's house, my mind was whirling like a generator. I had immediately grasped the concept that I might very well have been one of the children involved in the baby selling scandal. True, I no longer had any expectations about finding Mom, but this program whetted my appetite for more information about my family and renewed my belief in mankind.

Upon reaching home, I immediately called Denny. When Denny told me the scope of the scandal, I was speechless for the first time in my life. She told me what steps to take, and like a good little baby learning to walk, I responded to her motherly advice in earnest. In Denny Glad, I found a caring, organized, determined and intelligent wonder. I owe her

a huge debt that can never be calculated let alone
paid. She will be in my thoughts until my last moment on this earth. The only sad part about my relationship with Denny is that her late husband, Jerry,
is not here to see the fruition of his wife's life effort.

Denny told me it would take between two to
three weeks to receive my original birth certificate
in the mail. I made out the check I had been so reluc-
tant to write earlier. After a week went by, I began
checking my post office box. My spirits were high.

In the past, I had made the mistake of having
expectations that were unreal and unlikely to be met.
During my wait for the all-important letter, I worked
on making adjustments to my thinking. First of all, I
set my ultimate goals: 1. Find my real name. 2. Find
my father and his family. 3. Visit my mother's grave
and find her family. I also decided that I would not
count on developing a relationship with any of the
relatives I might find. My emphasis would simply
be on knowing who they are and letting them know
I exist. Anything else would be putting myself at risk
of having another episode of depression should our
meeting turn sour.

On February 11, I finally was in possession of
the letter I had been waiting for. It felt like Christmas morning! I drove home, not wanting to open the
envelope until I was in my own space.

Upon arriving home I moved slowly, relishing the prospects of the information, contained on the piece of paper, that might affect my destiny. The importance was double. Not only was the letter to possibly reveal the pathway to my biological family, but it perhaps would test my resolve to stop setting myself up for falls that resulted in depression. The ground began to swell like the ocean, so I sat down on an uncovered wire chair that hurt my butt. The pain helped focus me.

As my shaking hands slowly tore the seal on the envelope, I could feel the zephyrs of time rushing invisibly past. I knew immediately it was my birth certificate, because my check was not in the envelope. If the check had been returned, it would have meant that they could not locate my birth certificate.

"Please don't give me another weird name," I prayed as I pulled the paper from the envelope.

The birth certificate had a very dignified looking triple fold. The raised seal of the State of Tennessee greeted my anxious fingertips. I took one more deep breath. Tears of happiness rolled down my cheeks. "George Curtis," was the name that greeted my eyes. "What a beautiful name!" I thought. I felt like a football player who had just scored the winning touchdown at the Super Bowl. I tried to think of people who have the surname Curtis and only came up with Tony Curtis, the actor, and Mike Curtis, a great linebacker for the Baltimore Colts. Then my mind hit a blank space. My forehead wrinkled as I tried to fill the empty space with famous people named Curtis. My lack of success only caused me to smile. There was plenty of room for George Curtis.

I was mildly surprised to see the name George on my birth certificate as when I was adopted, it had been given to me as a middle name. My biological father's name was listed as John G. Curtis. I would later find out that the "G" stood for George. I would also discover that on my Baptismal Certificate, my middle name would be listed as John. there was a reason for this. The Greek system of naming children gives the first-born son his father's first name as his middle name. It struck me as ironic that both my adopted father and my biological father had the same first name.

In subsequent days, I found myself writing my name over and over in cursive like children do when they first learn to write their names. After a lifetime of writing one name, I knew it would take some time before writing my real name would become second nature.

The information provided on the certificate checked out. One other child was listed as having been born to my mother. That would be my sister. My birth took place at St. Joseph's Hospital, Memphis, Tennessee, on August 6, 1949. Unfortunately, the block where Mother's maiden name was supposed to be was occupied by Kathleen Reba Curtis. The clerk had made the mistake of putting down her married name instead of her maiden name. This deprived me of a very important piece of information I would need to locate my relatives on her side of the family.   .

My father's place of birth was listed as Washington, D.C., and my mother's place of birth was Camden, Tennessee. Mother was a housewife and father was unemployed.

One of my goals had been fulfilled. My real name had finally been disclosed to me. I was a little let down over the mistake concerning my mother's maiden name, but a reality check told me I was far from being on the road to depression. I called Denny to share my elation. She was truly happy for me, though both of us knew there was much more to be done. Denny told me she would try to obtain any juvenile records the court had made of me and would call me on the 28th of February with news. In order for Denny to have access to my records, I had to arrange for her to have Power of Attorney.

The person at the other end of the line on the morning of February 28 was, as I had expected, Denny Glad. Her maternal voice was assuring me of additional information. She had obtained a copy of my juvenile record and was sending it to me. A few days later I received the copy, twelve pages neatly written by Denny Glad. Thank God for people like Denny Glad. The following chapter is derived from the record she sent me.

CHAPTER TEN
The Juvenile Record

On August 6, 1949, a baby boy was born to John
G. Curtis and Kathleen Reba Kirk Curtis. The child
was delivered at St. Joseph's Hospital in Memphis,
Tennessee. Normally we think of the birth of a child
in joyous terms. The addition of a child to a family is
one of the happiest occasions in any couple's life.
Unfortunately, we cannot know the feelings of
Kathleen for her new child. We can speculate that
her emotions were happiness tempered with trepida-
tion for the future. The date gives us no clue as to the
reason for apprehension on the part of any mother
giving birth at this time. The war was over. The nation was entering a period of prosperity and wealth
such as had never before been seen in the history of
mankind. Truth, Justice and the American Way were
going to triumph. Every one said it was so. After all,
we had won the war and were the strongest nation in
the world both economically and militarily. Was
there, on this day of personal triumph, a cloud hanging over Kathleen Curtis?

Just before her thirteenth birthday, Officer
Boyle of the Memphis Police Department brought
Kathleen before the Juvenile Court. She was there
on charges of being a dependent child. Her father
had brought her to the Memphis Police Department

saying that her mom was deceased, and he was ill
and not able to take care of her. Acting Juvenile Court
Judge Featherstone committed Kathleen to St. Peter's
Orphanage.

Almost two years later Kathleen ran away and
was apprehended. Judge Kelley committed her to a
Catholic school for older girls called The Convent
of the Good Shepherd, where she spent the next three
years in the care of the nuns who ran the school. On
October 18, 1943, her aunt, Mrs. Hattie Craig, petitioned the Juvenile Court for her release. She was
unsuccessful at this time, because the convent had
recommended against it. Two years later, after a second petition by Mrs. Hattie Craig was filed, Judge
Kelley reviewed the case and released Kathleen to
her aunt. Thus ends the record of Kathleen's years
as a juvenile. There was no record available at this
time of my father, John.

On May 3, 1949, there is a record of a complaint made by my mother to the Juvenile court. It
was a complaint many mothers are familiar with even
today, non-support. My sister, Margaret Katherine
Curtis, had been born the previous year and Mom
was pregnant with me at the time. Judge Kelley, on
the basis of a Non-Support Warrant signed by my
mother, ordered Probation Officer Rosenbush to pursue the Non-Support Warrant. At the same time,
Judge Kelley ordered Probation Officer Martin to in-

vestigate Mom's living conditions and care of her
child.

Officer Rosenbush interviewed my mother on
May 5, and learned that she had met Dad at the Brass
Rail, a bar in Memphis, the previous Saturday night.
She had been sitting at a table with three or four
women and a marine when John came in. He accused
her of being with the marine and struck her in the
face with a glass before knifing the marine. Dad paid
a $50 forfeit after being arrested. I don't know what
went on before in their relationship, but this was to
be the end.

Mom was evicted from her apartment and
sought to place her daughter at St. Peter's. In addition, she felt a need to begin thinking about placing
her unborn baby for adoption. It is hard to blame
her. At 24 years of age she was a mother, pregnant
with a second child and without a home, husband or
income.

Dad's side of the story was a little different.
In response to a summons, he appeared at Juvenile
Court for a conference on May 5, 1949. He stated
that he was employed at Capitol Restaurant at 84 N.
Second Street at a wage of $35 per week. He said
that Mom was in the company of some sailors and
two other women at the Brass Rail on Saturday, April
30, when he tried to get her to go home with him.
The sailors intervened, and there was a fight. He

claimed he cut one of the sailors in self-defense. He agreed to pay $11.50 a week for the support of his wife and child, and he had no objection to Kathleen's plans for the children.

By the end of May, Mom had made arrangements for me to be delivered at St. Joseph's in the free clinic while St. Peter's cared for my sister. St. Joseph's and St. Peter's were both advised, presumably by welfare, that Mom planned to relinquish me for adoption. Sis took up residency in St. Peter's on the first of June, the day after my father's first support check arrived.

By the first of July, Mom was notifying Juvenile Court that I was overdue. I wasn't the only thing overdue. Dad wasn't paying the support money regularly and had said he was working and traveling with a circus. His latest payment was more than two weeks past due, Mom told the court.

By July 29, Mom found that Dad was working with his father at a bakery in Bluefield, W. Virginia and tried to have him arrested for non-payment of support money. It was not possible at that time to arrest Dad, but Officer Rosenbush promised to write an official letter demanding payment. Mom hung up then called back later to say never mind, she was going to hire a lawyer.

On August 6, 1949, doctors induced labor in my mother, and I was born. She named me George and told the court that she had changed her mind about my being adopted because Dad had called and asked her to join him in W. Virginia when she could. Mom was released from the hospital four days later with me and went to stay at Aunt Stella Scola's house.

Miss Shea of St. Peter's called to inquire why Mom had changed her mind about placing her children for adoption. When she was informed of her plans, Miss Shea complained that someone should pay for Katherine's care at St. Peter's. The answer given her was that Mom was receiving very little money from Dad. Mom was interviewed again by Officer Bloodworth. She stated that she wanted to keep both babies. She had heard about temporary room and board being offered for children at the Tennessee Children's Home Society. Officer Bloodworth contacted Miss Tann of TCHS, who agreed to take me for temporary care.

Officer Bloodworth took me to TCHS. My sister remained at St. Peter's. Miss Shea of St. Peter's was upset. She called the Juvenile Court to ask why I was not with my sister at St. Peter's. She also called at a later date to complain that my mother had not been to see my sister. She was told that Mom had gone to W. Virginia to see Dad and try to work something out between them.

In the meantime, Mom had complained that Dad was not sending money. She had taken a job as a waitress, but had to quit due to illness. She also saw to it that I would be baptized in the Catholic faith. St. Peter's wanted the rite postponed until Katherine and I could be baptized together, but Mom was afraid that St. Peter's wanted to get their hands on us so they could place both of us for adoption. What an irony this turned out to be!

Katherine spent Christmas that year with Mom at Mom's request. My godfather, Uncle Charlie, was kind enough to provide his home. Mom was still hoping to find a way of keeping us both, according to her statements in the Juvenile record. However, Miss Shea got busy again. She called Officer Bloodworth to insist that both Katherine and I be put in St. Peter's so that brother and sister could be together. Officer Bloodworth explained to her that Kathleen Curtis had made no such request. A week later Attorney B. J. Semmes called Officer Bloodworth saying he represented Mrs. Curtis who wanted me to be at St. Peter's to be with my sister on the condition that neither my sister nor I be placed for adoption. Officer Bloodworth patiently explained that no action could take place until Mrs. Curtis personally requested it. Mom called later that day to approve my move to St. Peter's. She said the nuns kept postponing the baptism until both children could be baptized together. This conversation occurred on 1/11/50. The very next day, Miss Georgia Tann called Juvenile Court to say that Monsignor Kearney would baptize me Sunday afternoon. If Mom wanted to attend, she (Miss Tann) would provide transportation to the service if Mom could be at the Tennessee Children's Home Society by 1:30 PM. Miss Tann was true to her word. She called Officer Bloodworth on 1/16 and told her I had been baptized the previous day, and Mrs. Curtis had attended but had seemed unfamiliar with the customs of the Catholic Church. Mom called later in the day to ask if the case could be brought immediately before Judge Kelley the next day.

On 1/17/50 every one showed up at court, every one except Miss Shea who said her presence was hardly necessary and she couldn't attend in any case. I find it interesting that Mom found it so important to call the case before the judge on the day after my baptism. It is also interesting that when in court she stated that she was afraid that I would be given away by TCHS and she now wanted me to be transferred to St. Peter's to be with my sister. One can only infer that on that ride from TCHS to the church with Miss Tann, an important conversation took place which changed my mother's whole outlook on who was trying to place me for adoption against her will. Judge Kelley had her own agenda. Coincidentally, it agreed with TCHS and Miss Tann. Both my sister and I were made wards of the court. I was to stay at TCHS, and

Sis was to stay at St. Peter's. The Juvenile record states that the care was to be "temporary care."

On the following day, Mr. B. J. Semmes, the man who claimed to be Mom's attorney but was actually the attorney for St. Peters, called and was informed of the decision. The way this all adds up in the record, I would guess that Miss Shea and Mr. B. J. Semmes knew something about TCHS my mother did not know until it was too late. Miss Shea, it seems, was not only trying to keep my sister and me together, but she and Mr. Semmes were trying to keep both of us out of the hands of TCHS and Miss Georgia Tann. The reason she did not appear in court on 1/17/50 may have had some thing to do with the fact that the presiding judge was Judge Kelley. The importance of this fact will be established a little later in this narrative.

Having a baby is a traumatic experience to begin with. When you add to that the breaking up of the family, the lack of money, the young age of my mother and the threat of losing the children, you have a situation that will rock the world of even the most stable person. According to some of my relatives on Mother's side, she was not stable at all. In the juvenile record, Mrs. Stella Scola, Mom's sister, told Officer Bloodworth in an interview that Mom behaved improperly after I was born. She had men in and out of the house, one of them a married man.

Mrs. Stella Scola asked officer Bloodworth if she could be given custody of me. Officer Bloodworth's reply was that I had not had any contact with the family and wouldn't know any of them. Officer Bloodworth further stated that it was best for me to be left at TCHS to be placed for adoption. I suppose that under this reasoning you would have to agree that strangers would have to be better than members of my own family because they would know me better.

The situation escalated after Easter. Mom had asked Juvenile Court if she could have the children over Easter and the court replied that she had to apply to the respective institutions for permission. There is no record as to whether or not she was able to do this, but on 5/6/50 she was arrested for hanging around beer joints. The charge was disorderly conduct. Later, in December of 1951, she was arrested on charges of prostitution and selling dope. I make no excuses for my mother and the way she lived her life, but I do want it known that she was my mom. Even though I never knew her, I still love her and appreciate the fact that she brought me into this world. I also appreciate that she did at least try to keep my sister and me.

No one can say what might have happened if Kathy and I had stayed with Mom, but it can be said that some very powerful forces kept us apart.

Mother's irresponsibility, her sister's witness against her, my dad's irresponsibility, Miss Tann of TCHS and Camile Kelley and Officer Bloodworth of Juvenile Court—all these elements had a part to play in the way my sister and I would live the rest of our lives. On 9/15/50, Georgia Tann died of pneumonia, a complication of the cancer she had been carrying in her body for a year or more. She had been ill for some time, and I am convinced that her weakened condition and her unwillingness to delegate any of her authority prevented her from moving quickly to have me adopted. After Miss Tann died, Judge Camille Kelley resigned. However, their actions were to continue to have an effect on Kathy and myself for many years.

After the death of Miss Tann and the resignation of Judge Kelley, the Tennessee Children's Home Society was allowed to continue in a limited capacity. Part of the reason for this was that it was reorganized and there was the question of what to do with the children left there. Eventually, TCHS even obtained a license. My mother was in and out of town—neither the court nor her relatives were able to keep in touch with her. Attorney Semmes petitioned the court to declare us abandoned children. Dad was overseas in the army. Mom was finally reached and consented for us to be placed for adoption. The surrender papers were obtained a short time later from both Mom and Dad. In the meantime, I had joined my sister at St. Peter's. When Mom signed the surrender papers, she realized she was in no position to provide a proper home for us children. Since John, my dad, had already signed the papers she thought it was time for my sister and me to be placed for adoption so we could have the kind of family life she never had, and the love and attention we deserved. How could she have known what would ultimately happen?

Of course, what happened was that John and Doris came looking for a little girl to round out their perfect family. They fell in love with Kathy and would take no substitutes. When the nuns were told of their choice, they informed John and Doris that she was part of a set. In other words, Kathy came with a brother and the two were inseparable. This is how I became the two-for-one child.

In a way, this was good because I was able to grow up with one blood relative and had the pleasure of knowing my sister who is not only a very lovely person, but a kindhearted one as well. The down side—well, I think the reader knows by now what that was.

I have long thought that the adoption laws in this country should be changed. No system is foolproof, but we can certainly do better by children than we have done in the past or are doing right now. But that is not the end of it. We not only need to do a better job with the children who are to be adopted, but we need to do right by all our children. I've heard many people say, "My kids come first," and this is the way it should be. But for the most part, from what I have seen anyway, children are second class citizens—the largest minority in America. Children aren't old enough to vote. There are few adult voices on their side, so when legislation affecting them is being considered, their needs seem to be pushed aside by adult wants and needs. I'm not just talking about legislation, either. I'm talking about the everyday things as well. Children are so small and inexperienced compared to adults that often they are pushed aside and not listened to. Adults forget they were once children. They forget, or don't know in the first place, that children are vested with a certain wisdom unpolluted by experience.

When I decided at age four to find my biological family, I figured to achieve this goal by telling every one whom would listen that I was adopted. I felt that someday a connection would be made. Thirty-eight years later it paid off. Children can see solutions to some problems clearly and with ease. Adults would miss those same solutions if you led them to the answers. Because of their lack of experience, we call them "dumb kids" and leave it at that.

Our country is paying for this even as I write.

We have hundreds of thousands, possibly millions, of dysfunctional adults who are now and will be until they die, a liability to our civilization. It doesn't end there. Those dysfunctional adults will have children. It has been proven that dysfunctional adults produce dysfunctional children who in turn grow up to be a liability to themselves and society. How do we propose to handle the situation? Do we build more prisons to keep them off the streets?

I recently saw a clip on Sixty Minutes describing a prison program going on in one state. The program is considered very successful. It consists of offering prisoners a free opportunity to get an education. They can even get a college degree. It was noted in the program that most convicted lawbreakers have little or no education. There was not one word to indicate that anyone was interested in giving away free education to kids to keep them out of the big house.

For the most part, we just want to warehouse those who break the laws, just like we would rather punish our children than spend time thinking of ways to help them learn from their mistakes. We would rather provide prisons than schools and, we would rather give punishment than education.

For my part, I would like to see a new cabinet seat created, an advocate for children. The advocate's voice should be listened to above every one else. In addition, I feel we should establish a savings account for each child in the United States at the time they first enter school. One thousand dollars should be added to it each year that they complete a grade level successfully. When the child graduates from high school, the money would be available for them to use to further their education in college or trade school. If they do not successfully graduate from college, the money would, after a time, revert back to the general fund. This would give children a chance to see the value of their education. In addition, each child would have a start on the money needed to educate themselves further in a world that demands higher education and training for its work force. These children who take advantage of this program would probably not wind up in our overcrowded prison system.

Think about these last paragraphs carefully. We need a program like this one to get our nation back on track so we will be able to compete with the rest of the world, and so we will not become a nation of prisons.

CHAPTER ELEVEN
The Tomb of Doom

This chapter is included for a couple of reasons, the first being that the Tennessee Children's Home Society played a big part in my life. Another reason is that it was a major influence in many lives and needs to be further examined. The last reason is that some of what went on in Memphis at TCHS helps explain some of the events recorded in my juvenile file.

To begin with, Edward Hull Crump otherwise known as "Boss" Crump dominated politics in the state of Tennessee, at this time. Crump rose to power in the 20's and over the years constructed a powerful political machine. Crump's machine did not begin to crumble until the late 40's. Thanks to the Crump machine, TCHS was able to operate, and when the end came, though Boss Crump was in decline, the machine prevented a full accounting from being possible.

Much of what we know can never be proven in a court of law, due to the efforts of Abe Waldauer, a lieutenant in the Crump machine. When the final investigation started, it was Waldauer who was seen removing boxes of documents from TCHS. These documents were recovered thirty days later with many of the most important papers missing. The guilty parties were never brought to trial. The following are some of the major players in the scandal.

Abe Waldauer began as an attorney for Crump in 1932. He was put in charge of voter irregularities. That year he defended the Crump organization against charges by a losing candidate that supporters had been intimidated. Eventually, he became the liaison between Governor Browning and Crump during Browning's first term. When Browning acted to reduce Crump's power, Waldauer sided with Crump despite a longtime friendship with Browning that began during W.W.I. When the walls of TCHS began to crumble under scrutiny of an investigation by Robert Love Taylor, special investigator appointed by Governor Browning, Abe Waldauer was the attorney for TCHS. Despite the promise given by the board of directors of TCHS that no records would be removed, Waldauer was observed removing documents by a private investigator hired by Taylor. It took thirty days and a court injunction to get the records back. As Robert Taylor notes in his report to Governor Browning, a large portion of the checks had been removed.

Camille Kelley was appointed judge of the newly created Juvenile Court in Memphis. Rowlet Paine, mayor of Memphis and a Crump supporter appointed her. After the appointment, her qualifications were called into question as she had never practiced law. A bill was rammed through the state legislature, courtesy of Crump, which allowed her to serve without having practiced law. In addition, she served in her post for 30 years unopposed in every election. She was forced to resign November 10, 1950 in order to prevent an investigation that may have resulted in her prosecution for crimes related to the TCHS scandal. Kelley was listed in the juvenile records as the presiding judge in the proceedings concerning me.

Georgia Tann was the person in direct control of TCHS. When the end came, she was the one who took all the blame. It was easy since she died just two days after the scandal was exposed. Tann was very close to Judge Kelley, and the two used some very effective tactics to procure babies for the operation. When a review of Tann's estate was done after her death, it was found that she had money and jewelry in a safe deposit box and real estate holdings she couldn't possibly have paid for with her meager salary as a public servant.

Mrs. Carolyn Bloodworth was appointed probation officer of Kelley's court. Her name appeared frequently in my juvenile record and she was directed by Kelley to pick up children Kelley had decided were to be made wards of the court. The evidence against her is mostly by association. However, she did a fair job of trying to discourage my aunt, Stella

Scola, from seeking custody.

There were doubtless many others who participated in the TCHS black market baby ring, but their
names and both time and an excellent cover-up have
buried the evidence against them. Robert Taylor was
a supporter of Governor Browning and was appointed
special investigator of the TCHS scandal. Due to his
efforts, much of the scandal was uncovered and
Kelley resigned from office under threat of the whole
mess being taken to court. Unfortunately, this move
prevented the full disclosure that would have come
had the case made it to the courtroom. Taylor was
empowered to investigate Tanns last two years of
atrocities.

The operation of a successful black market
baby-selling scheme depends on a supply of babies.
In some cases, the babies were obtained from unwed mothers. TCHS advertised throughout the South
as a haven for unwed mothers where they and their
child would be cared for and medical facilities would
be provided for the birth. Some of these mothers gave
up their babies willingly. Many were coerced.

It was easy to trick young mothers into giving
up their children. Illegitimate children were considered a scandal in themselves at this time in our history. In many cases the women were illiterate which
made it impossible for them to know what they were
signing when they were asked to sign important pa-

pers. The women would be told that they were signing papers for temporary placement when in reality
the documents were surrender papers. Some women
were actually told they would be allowed to visit their
children and would not find out until they tried to
see the children that they were gone from their lives
forever. Some of these women were told their child
had died. In other cases they were told the children
were already adopted. Many times, the mothers
would simply be declared unfit by the juvenile court
headed by Camille Kelley, and the children would
simply be taken away.

Troubled families were also an important
source of babies for TCHS. In these cases, Judge
Kelley worked in tandem with Tann. Tann would
notify Kelley whenever she found a family where a
father had lost his job or there was a divorce or other
trouble. Kelley would have the children picked up.
The case would then go to her court. Tann sent relatives and friends to scour the county in search of
troubled families with young, adoptable children and
to spread the information to hospitals that TCHS was
the only organization able to provide legal adoptions.
Doctors, nurses, other hospital staff and lawyers were
told these lies. Many believed them. In addition to
the above methods for obtaining babies, there were
cases where babies were taken from patients in asy-
lums for the mentally ill. A phony history was then

written. The baby's history was crafted to impress a couple that TCHS had selected to adopt the baby.

With the supply side well stocked with babies, the black market scheme could not have taken place if there had been no demand. The demand was filled, at first, by placing ads in the local newspaper, during the Christmas season, that read, "Christmas Babies for Adoption." These babies were not sold for profit. The profit taking came later. According to Linda Tollett Austin, there was no intention of starting a baby-selling ring in the beginning. The profit taking came later. Ms. Austin points out that Georgia Tann and Judge Kelley did some good work in their early years, and it was only later that they became corrupted. Both women had nationwide recognition for their work with juveniles. Hollywood was even interested in making a movie about Kelley just before the news about the scandal broke. A TV series was started. One episode was completed, but both Kelley and the director died before any more could be accomplished.

A few of the babies were sold to celebrities. June Allyson and Dick Powell, Joan Crawford, Smiley Burnette were some of the celebrities on the list who adopted babies through TCHS. In addition, prominent local officials participated by adopting children from TCHS. Many of the adoptive parents came from out of state, California and New York in particular. All of them had the money to pay the price requested.

New York and California both had laws requiring a person to be married to adopt a child. California had an additional law that made it illegal to adopt children out of state. There was not only money in both states, but also many prospective parents who felt blocked by the bureaucracy. Tann broke the law to cut red tape. To these people, Tann was a temporary heroine.

Before I break down the price to show how money was made, I wish to remind the reader that the dollar was worth more back in the forties than it is worth today. A hundred dollars back then was a small fortune. Today it represents but a token. The clients were charged $721.47 for a baby placed in California. Placement in New York was slightly higher. That cost included the home investigation ($168.72), attorneys' fees ($202.75) and delivery ($350.00). The actual cost to TCHS for all of these services was only $100.00. Many of the adoptive parents did not know they were participating in a baby-selling ring. Those who knew had it used against them as a leverage for special favors. Those who only suspected kept quiet fearing that calling attention to their adopted child would result in the adoption being declared illegal and the surrender of their child. In addition to the charges listed above, adoptive parents were solicited for donations to the building fund. The grateful parents were an easy mark as many had already tried other routes to adopt a child and had failed. Some people were said to have given TCHS $1,000 gifts, gifts that never went for the purpose intended. TCHS also had funding from the state. The funding began in 1915 at a rate of $120,000 every two years.

Most of the children were delivered either to California or New York. The children were taken four or five at a time. Their caretaker rented a hotel room and kept the babies there. Appointments were set up with the adoptive parents at half-hour intervals in the lobby of the hotel. In this way, TCHS was able to maximize their profits.

According to Robert Taylor's report to J. O. McMahan, Commissioner of Public Welfare of the State of Tennessee, there were other irregularities much worse than those listed above. Babies were transported to their new homes or taken into TCHS as soon as possible after birth. This resulted in the deaths of several babies and sickness among many. Some of the children were returned because they were sick and in poor condition when the adoptive parents received them. There were many parents in California who complained to the California Department of Welfare about the condition of babies received in their homes.

Andrew age 14

One-eyed Brian, Sister
Kathy and Golden Boy

Cousin Rosali Owens, Denny Glad, and I at Applebees
Restaurant, Memphis Tennessee, 1992

Doris & John Bubnes, De-
troit, Michigan, 1954

Kathy age 7

Mom Curtis circa 1940s

Big Sister and Little
Brother, St. Peter's
Orphanage, 1951

Cousin Rosalie and Ollie
Owens, March 1992
Memphis, Tennessee

Sister Kathy's High School
Graduation 1967

Jennifer Bubnes, graduation
1988

John George Curtis 1945

The Davis Girls, Baby & Josephine and me. 1991

Uncle Tony and Aunt Stella, Easter Sunday 1962, Memphis, Tennessee

Dad and I, November
1993, Norfolk, Virgina,
Stonehouse Restaurant
and Lounge.

Brian (the author) at age 3

Alice, Dad, and I, Norfolk, Virgina, 1993

Judge Sam Bates, a judge in Memphis at this time, requested a thorough investigation of TCHS. One of his charges was that babies were taken from the local Methodist Hospital in perfect condition and given such inadequate care that many died and many more were taken back to the hospital in an emaciated condition. There is recorded in Judge Bate's report that four different doctors, one of whom worked at TCHS, complained of a lack of medical examinations before placement. Babies placed for adoption were unfit (in one case the child had congenital syphilis). Director Tann countermanded doctor's orders. Nurses drunk on duty, deaths of babies going unrecorded so no one knew about them, and, one incident of diarrhea breaking out in the nursery and killing as many as 50 children, were overlooked. Despite the doctor's orders, the home continued to receive children during the epidemic. In addition, the children were not given the care or the medication he ordered. The doctor who worked at TCHS resigned his post after filing a complaint. Tann should have been prosecuted for murdering these babies.

The care of the children was sloppy at best. Those who did not reside in the TCHS receiving home went to boarding homes where the care was not any better. The boarding homes were run by people who were not educated or trained in running them and were not investigated as to their fitness for this occupation. The homes themselves were not inspected for fitness of habitation. The adoptive couples were not thoroughly investigated and no follow-up was done to see how the new family was adjusting. Many of the children's records were tampered with or simply fictionalized. This resulted in the return of some babies who were born retarded or with other genetic defects. Medical records of the children were incomplete, pure fiction, or nonexistent.

A Mrs. Browne detailed another crime committed by TCHS. Her child was born while her husband was unemployed. Her husband, thinking that TCHS was a state agency, applied there for help. Miss Tann told her TCHS would provide temporary care for the child until the family got back on its feet. All she had to do was to sign a little agreement. When Mrs. Browne refused to sign, Miss Tann called in the juvenile court, and the family had to flee the state in order to keep their child. Kelley and Tann were both responsible for breaking up families which could have been kept together with a little help. Of course, giving them a little help would not have been profitable. Taking their children was.

There were others who were not so lucky. There was one case where a man and wife divorced. The woman was left with seven children, three of whom were taken care of by friends. Miss Tann discovered the children and declared that they were in

the care of unfit parties. Judge Kelley ordered them
to be placed in the custody of the juvenile court and
transferred to TCHS. In the meantime, the man re-
married and had two more children by his new wife.
During her stay in the hospital with the second child,
she sought help with the oldest. A representative of
TCHS went to the hospital to offer the woman a place
to board the child until she was able to take care of it
again. They also were there to attempt to coerce her
into giving up the youngest baby for adoption. When
that did not work, both children were declared wards
of the state and taken from her and her husband.
When the husband tried to get the children back,
Kelley charged the man with raping his daughter and
threatened to bring charges against him if he inter-
fered with the placement of the children.

The couple moved to New Orleans to avoid
prosecution. The woman returned and hired a lawyer to try to recover the children. While in the hall of
the courthouse, she was approached by Judge Kelly
of the Juvenile Court, and threatened with indictment
by the Attorney General. According to the report of
Robert Love Taylor to Governor Browning, this case
is borne out by both the records of the court combined with the testimony of witnesses who are be-
lievable.

There were many stories like this surfacing
over the years about the Juvenile Court and TCHS.

In many of the cases the parents never saw their children again. Families were unnecessarily broken up and scattered to the four winds. Lives were shattered, and faith in this country's legal system was lost.

Where did the money go? There exists no evidence that anyone other than Georgia Tann profited financially from the operations at TCHS. Some of the records that were removed by the attorney for TCHS, Abe Waldauer, as witnessed covertly by a private investigator hired by Robert Taylor, doubtless contained the information we seek. Common sense tells us that to run a scheme as organized as this one was, it would take more than one or two people to do the work. Very few of us are willing to work for free, and I submit that no one who is doing illegal work will walk away without their share. As I said before, it is easy to place the blame on a dead person.

An important question to emerge from all of this is how were they able to do it? Again, the effort was very organized. Some played their parts unwittingly, but others must have known what they were accomplishing.

On May 15, 1924, Georgia Tann moved to Memphis where she was placed in charge of TCHS. At this time TCHS handled children from ages seven to eighteen. In December of 1929, TCHS had 25 children ready for adoption. She had applications for these children but considered them mediocre homes for the children at best. She glanced down at the throngs of Christmas shoppers, and her Christmas babies scheme was born. Each day until the end of the year, she placed an advertisement in the Press Scimitar with a picture of a child waiting for adoption. The program was such a success that it continued through the 1940's. It has already been mentioned that TCHS received $60,000 biennially from the state fund. In addition they received $6,000 yearly from the Community Fund. All the workers' salaries and all the expenses of the organization were paid with this money. It was not enough. In 1933, the agency had a budget deficit of $1,876.50. By the late 1930's, Georgia Tann was herself profiting from the sale of children.

The jurisdiction over adoptions in Tennessee was with the county, circuit, and chancery courts, but in the major cities such as Memphis and Nashville, Juvenile Courts had authority and could consent to adoptions if children were abandoned. The Department of Public Welfare was created in 1937. All child welfare services were administered through the Child Welfare Division of the Department of Public Welfare. The Department was hampered by a shortage of staff, having only sixteen child welfare workers for the whole state.

A statute created in 1937 allowed non-residents of Tennessee to adopt children from any child-caring institution or agency. This statute, passed by Crump supporters, was one of the laws which allowed the baby selling scheme to exist. First of all, Tennessee was not where the money was located. California and New York filled that bill nicely. Secondly, some of the money was made on the transportation costs of one baby when several were transported at a reduced cost per head.

Another statute was created in 1941 allowing the surrender of a child to legally take place before a notary public rather than before a judge. This meant a judge would not be present to ask questions of the unwed or destitute mother so it could be certain she was surrendering her child without coercion. The Tennessee adoption laws in the 40's also allowed the courts to consent to the adoption of an abandoned child *in loco parentis*. Individuals, specifically doctors, nurses, midwives, hospital officials and officers of unauthorized institutions were forbidden to participate in the placement of children. The Child Welfare League and the State Department referred cases for permanent placement to TCHS. In 1941, the Child Welfare League investigated TCHS and pulled their certification. No longer would they refer cases to TCHS. By 1945, the Department of Welfare was in direct competition with TCHS, and it became apparent to workers in the Department that the adoption practices of TCHS were irregular.

The competition between welfare and TCHS was stiff enough for Abe Waldauer to make a complaint to Weber C. Tuley, a district Attorney-General, that the Department of Public Welfare should not be allowed to place children for adoption in violation of Section 4737 of the code of Tennessee. This section of the law forbids private persons and officers of unauthorized institutions from placing children for adoptions. Tuley ruled against Waldauer. Both TCHS and the Department of Public Welfare continued to place children.

From 1945 until 1950, the Shelby County delegation under the control of Crump was able to block or water down adoption reform proposals. In 1945, for instance, the legislature was finally able to outlaw the operation of boarding homes without licenses. TCHS, however, was exempted from this law. Two more proposals were made in 1947, but two legislators from Crump's Shelby County delegation had the bills successfully tabled and in effect prevented their consideration by the full legislature for the rest of the year. A weak bill was passed which allowed the Department of Public Welfare to care for and place children for adoption, but did not allow them the power to supervise children in the home. Another bill was introduced in 1948 and endorsed by TCHS. This statute was meant only to ensure that a more liberal law was not passed. Later in the year a better law was passed allowing the prospective parents to be investigated. The bill gave the mother of birth 30 days to change her mind after the surrender of her child. Giving the presiding judge the responsibility of protecting the records also ensured confidentiality. In 1949, the Wooten Bill was passed. a portion of this bill restricted out-of-state adoptions by having them cleared with the Department of Public Welfare. By some accounts inept clerks left the above provision out of the bill erroneously. By other accounts the important provision of the bill was stolen. However it happened, the black market baby selling ring won another round.

Two days before the death of Miss Tann, the investigation of TCHS was made public. In his report to the governor, Robert Taylor estimated that Miss Tann profited in excess of $500,000. This is a substantial amount of money, even by today's standards. The adoption ring was able to continue from the late 30's to 1950 because of wide support in the Crump organization, support that opposed, stalled and reportedly stole legislation that would have reformed Tennessee's adoption laws preventing their operation from continuing.

All of the money that was made was not accounted for by any means. An average of $650 was made per child. There were, as near as we can tell, between 1,016 and 1,500 children placed for adoption out of state by TCHS between 1940 and 1950. By some accounts the number of children was at least twice as high as this. The total comes to between $660,400 and $975,000. This does not count the "gifts" to the building fund some of which were as much as $1,000. It also does not count the money made from children whose records were lost or destroyed.

Most of us know that the money was not very important when stacked up against the pain and suffering caused by the operation of the baby-selling ring. One might argue that there were some good homes found for children who needed them, but according to Taylor these were coincidental. For the most part, the operations of, "The Tomb of Doom", were not in the best interests of the children. The real question is, how many people were hurt? How many victims were there? How many dreams were destroyed? Only God knows.

This is a question we can never fully answer. There were families broken up, fathers and mothers who would never see their children again, sisters and brothers who would never see each other again. There were the children who died because of lack of proper care or because they were placed too soon after birth and those traumatized because of their treatment or because of losing their biological families. Add to this the children who were put into homes not fit or not right for them. Some of these homes were abusive homes. The abused children who came out of them became abusive as adults, and expanded the list of victims to their friends, spouses, children, and themselves. They lacked the proper socialization that allows most of us to get along with society in general. As a result, they committed crimes against other people. We must remember that abusive treatment is like a chain stretching across generations. Today, there are still people who are being made victims of the TCHS scandal. Also, we must remember the adoptive parents who waited so long for a child, who prayed to God that they might receive one and then received a child. They were unprepared to deal with a child with an altered past, a child with no medical records, either physical or mental, to help right the wrongs. How did they feel having to return this child? How much damage did it do to their lives?

It is certain the list of victims is in the tens of thousands, possibly hundreds of thousands. It does not end here. Linda Tollett Austin, in her dissertation, "Babies For Sale: The Tennessee Children's Home Adoption Scandal", has researched the problem. She found that at the same time TCHS was operating, five other black market baby adoption rings were also in operation. The locations of these adoption rings were Montreal, Canada; New York City,

New York; Chicago, Illinois; Duluth, Minnesota, Norman, Oklahoma and Texarkana, Texas. If TCHS produced so many victims, how many did these five additional adoption rings create? How many victims did adoption rings we have no knowledge of create? They could number in the millions. This chain has to be broken before it does any more damage to our society, to our world.

I have often heard the question "What is wrong with our country? What is wrong with the world?" A partial answer lies in the way we treat our children, all of our children. In her report to J. O. McMahan, Commissioner, Department of Public Welfare, Ms. Vallie S. Miller, Supervisor of Adoptions on the Tennessee Children's Home Society said, "The large number of draft rejeçts during World War II dramatized how ineffectively the states had been in dealing with problems of child health and protection." Does it really take a world war to point out that we have not succeeded in raising our children properly? Does it take a world war to tell us that we have not raised children fit enough even for cannon fodder? Has anything changed since then?

Today we have some people with more money and possessions than they will have time to spend or use in their lifetimes. They live lives surpassing the lives of kings of old, in comfort, wealth and power. Yet many of these same people are out there grabbing more and leaving the care of their children to baby-sitters and the schools, or military academies. We have millions of others who are single parents or families where both parents have to work so hard just to keep food on the table that they have no time or energy for their children. These children are entrusted to the schools or baby-sitters if they are lucky. If they are not lucky, the kids run unsupervised in the streets. What kind of a society are we? Is this how we are to raise the future of our country or doesn't anyone care anymore?

I am not saying that we can legislate a good family for all children. This would be impossible in any society and unthinkable in a free society that places such value on individuality. We can make rules to favor and promote good parenting. We can think of our children when we make major decisions. We can work on an individual level to make choices favorable to our own family and its structure. We can also incorporate values into our lives that place the family higher than the pervasive greed that infects our society.

Raising children is not just providing them with material things or opportunities. It is much more than any of us are able to realize before we actually have the responsibility of children, and more than many of us realize by the time our grandchildren arrive.

To raise a successful field of wheat, a farmer prepares the land carefully and chooses the seed with care as well, for he knows that all seeds are not the same. He then chooses the time and plants the seed in the soil, making sure that there is enough water to germinate it. As the seedling pushes through the soil, the farmer tends it, taking out the weeds and providing the moisture needed to make it grow, checking for pests and disease, keeping away the birds and chasing the cows from the field. He does all this because there is no second chance. If his crop fails, he may be ruined. So he does what he must to make the plants grow strong and large knowing that if he does, the yield will be high and his family will be fed.

We need to give the same care to our children. Schools and baby-sitters cannot do what parents can and should do for their children in the form of nurturing and education. Sadly, the above mentioned conditions apply for most of us, and it appears impossible to break the chain. But break the chain we must for our children are our future and if they are not taken care of correctly, in the next century will find our country's amber waves of grain withered by drought and disease and devoured by pests.

CHAPTER TWELVE
In the Shadow of the Tomb

Considering the scope of the operation, much more was going on at TCHS than ever was accounted for. Recall that at the beginning of the juvenile record, my mother was touched by the forces of TCHS. When she first came in contact with the Juvenile Court, her case was handled by acting Juvenile Judge Featherstone. The second time, when she ran away, Judge Camille Kelley who has been connected to Georgia Tann heard her case. Mother had been at St. Peter's Orphanage. She was transferred to The Convent of the Good Shepherd.

When mother was taken before the Juvenile Court the first time, TCHS was in business. Why wasn't she sent to TCHS to be sold? A possible answer lies in her age. She was in her teens at the time. It is much harder to place children in their teens than it is to place babies or infants. If this was the case, then why was Mother not put in the custody of her aunt when she petitioned for custody in 1943? After all, she was 18 at the time. Why wait until she was 20 before releasing her?

The nuns at the Convent of the Good Shepherd are on record as saying that she was not ready to be released. This very well could have been true. However, knowing the scheming going on to separate children from their parents so they could be placed for adoption, it is also possible that there was a plan to increase the available number of babies by creating situations in which those babies would be conceived and born in Tennessee where TCHS would have ready access to them. This is all speculation, of course. We do not know what connection, if any, the Convent had with TCHS. To my knowledge, no information has come to light suggesting TCHS used young women in this way. We do know that all the principles in the TCHS scandal were intelligent, that is attested to by the fact that they operated for so long without anyone getting caught. Intelligent people tend to be more than mere opportunists. They tend to create situations to benefit themselves rather than wait for them to develop. Still, we are delving into speculation.

Miss Shea, the social worker at St. Peter's, had a part to play in all of this. She was the person whose insistence that both my sister and I belonged together at St. Peter's caused my mother to think that St. Peter's had plans of placing the two of us for adoption. When trying to convince Mother that the place for both of us was at St. Peter's and making her opinion on our case known to the court did not work, Miss Shea tried the attorney trick of using St. Peter's attorney to pose as my mother's attorney. She then demanded that I be sent to St. Peter's with my sister.

When nothing she did was effective in separating me from TCHS, she did not attend the final Juvenile Court appearance that decided where my sister and I would be temporarily placed. Her exact words were that she, "hardly thought her presence was necessary." Miss Shea knew it would be a waste of time since Judge Kelley was the presiding judge. Miss Shea and St. Peter's lawyer, B. J. Semmes, knew the score. However, Attorney B. J. Semmes called Juvenile Court the next day to confirm the outcome.

The sisters at St. Peter's had been using my baptism as a possible trump to play against TCHS. They held off the baptism of my sister so that she and I could be baptized together. Georgia Tann saw to it that this card was never played by setting up a baptismal for me through Msgr. Kearney, who was on the Board of Directors at TCHS and the reigning prelate for the Memphis area. They knew that if transportation were provided, my mother would probably attend. What more fitting escort could she have than Miss Tann?

Miss Tann apparently had something to say to Mom as they rode in the back seat of the shiny black Packard owned by Miss Tann. We don't know what she said, but it probably went something like this: "You can keep the older child if you allow us to find a home for the baby." As has been pointed out in the chapter, "Tomb of Doom," this was a line used previously with other mothers.

The baptism was on Sunday. According to the juvenile record, mother called the court Monday morning and asked that the Juvenile Court immediately hear her case. She was probably relieved when she heard the voice on the other end of the line tell her it would be possible on the next day. But then she didn't know that Judge Camille Kelley and Georgia Tann were working together.

The same day Mother called the court, Miss Tann filed her report on the baptism. Her comment about Mom not being familiar with Catholic customs was clearly designed to shed some doubt on Mom. It could be nothing but a lie. How could Mother spend two years living at St. Peter's and five more years at the Convent of the Good Shepherd and not know the customs of the church?

We know my mother did not want to relinquish Sis and me at this time, because when she went to court, she testified she knew I was being well cared for at TCHS, but was afraid I would be given away. She wanted me transferred to St. Peter's so I could be with my sister. Presiding Juvenile Court Judge Kelley denied her request even though St. Peter's was willing to take me. It would have been just as easy for Kelley to let me go to St. Peter's. Why didn't she? Sis was allowed to stay at St. Peter's. Mom had originally placed her there, and it might have caused a conflict between St. Peter's and Juvenile Court had Sis been ordered to move to TCHS.

Seven months later, Officer Bloodworth interviewed Mrs. Stella Scola, Mom's sister. Stella told the officer Mom had not been acting properly while she stayed at her house after I was born. She went on to tell about the time she visited my mother in the hospital when Mom was cut in the face with a broken glass while at a bar. She further told of Mom's exploits as a dice girl in a nightclub, going to jail, and having men in and out of her home. Her appraisal of Mother was that she loved her, but Mom was not the proper person to care for her children. Damning evidence. She went on to ask if she could be given custody of the children. At this point Officer Bloodworth nixed the idea on the grounds that there had been no contact between me and the rest of my family and that it was best for me to be adopted through TCHS. Why wasn't I given to someone who cared about me and was related to me rather than a stranger? The answer was TCHS and Judge Kelley wanted to use me as they had used other children. One month after this interview, the investigation of TCHS was begun and Gerogia Tann died. Judge Kelley resigned about a month later to avoid being investigated for possible criminal prosecution. The juvenile records show that Aunt Stella Scola had several contacts with the Juvenile Court after the death of Georgia Tann, but no further attempt to gain custody of my sister and myself is noted in the juvenile record. I don't think that there is any question that life for my sister and I would have been significantly different had our relatives been allowed to adopt us out of love for their own blood. Instead, we were allowed to be adopted by John and Doris Bubnes who wished to "round out" a perfect family.

The removal of a large box of important records from TCHS by Abe Waldauer during the course of the investigation may have had an effect on my life. Was it just checks that were removed? The records were missing for thirty days. That was plenty of time to go through and change or remove any records that might have proved damning to other participants in the TCHS scandal. Was it during this time that my health records from TCHS were lost?

Perhaps there weren't any health records kept of me while I stayed at TCHS or they had been destroyed before Waldauer removed the records. These were both common practices at the, "Tomb of Doom."

The scar on my leg is from a serious burn that occurred when I was very young. My health records from St. Peter's do not mention anything about a serious injury. My health records, after I was adopted, do not mention the injury. I have to conclude that my leg was burned while I was at TCHS. I may never know exactly what caused the burn.

Shortly after I received my birth certificate and those of my biological mother and father and the above juvenile record, I approached my sister. She explained to me that when she was very young, Doris had told her that Mom was "a lady of the night." She also showed me the adoption papers Doris had recently sent her. Doris had known the story all along and had let Sis know but had kept it from me. Her only response to my questions about my origin were stories she made up about a baby selling ring in the state of Michigan that never existed and a lie about Mother kidnapping me and being caught by the authorities in Chicago. The key to the truth I had labored so long to expose had been within reach all those years, stored in a closet in the home I grew up in.

It is clear that I was marked for sale by TCHS. It is also clear that my life and my sister's life were forever affected by the refusal of Juvenile Court, headed by Camille Kelley, to place my sister and me with relatives who wanted us.

Part II: Life as George
The evil of man quieted the rapture in the
young boy's heart. But strong was the love between
boy and God.

CHAPTER THIRTEEN
First Contact

Attitude is a state of mind. For forty years I was
constantly made to feel by John and Doris and all
the other people around me that I had a bad attitude
and that I was never going to amount to anything
because of it. I could not understand what was happening to me. Everything I did was wrong. I was
hurt and could find no one to tell me how to ease the
pain. I was enslaved for forty years by people whose
own bad attitudes were shaping my life for me. But I
survived because I had fallen in love with God, and
my God was not mean.   In the Old Testament of the
Bible, God spoke to Abraham. God told Abraham
that for four hundred years his people would live in
the land of Egypt enslaved by Pharaoh. Abraham's
greatest descendent, Moses would lead the descen-
dants of Abraham out of Egypt on the final day.
Moses, in the Egyptian language, means one drawn
from the river.

Moses led his people into the desert where they
wandered for forty years. Only two of the children

of Abraham survived to cross into Canaan, Caleb and
Joshua. Joshua in Hebrew means Jesus, the chosen
one. For seven days the Israelites walked around the
walls of Jericho. At given intervals they would blow
their horns as loud as they could. On the seventh day,
the walls of Jericho fell.

For three weeks, February 11 until the 28th, I
had my original birth certificate in my possession.
The unfortunate part was that my mother's maiden
name was not on it. Instead, a gross error had been
committed. Her married name was all I would learn
from this document. The suspense of these three
weeks was torturous. After forty years, I had reached
the Promised Land only to find a wall blocking my
way.

I instructed a notary public to give Denny Glad
the power of attorney as she had requested. This action would allow her to open my juvenile records.
We were certain that the information needed to find
my family would come from these records. I could-
n't wait.

To break down the walls of bureaucracy, I got
on the horn. I called Social Security to find my dad.
I felt that if I went to Social Security with the name
of my dad, they would be sympathetic to my cause.

The phone call led to a personal visit at the
local Social Security office. The worker who attended
me was cordial and sympathetic. I gave her my fa-

ther's name and place of birth. When she asked for his birth date, I was only able to give her September 1926. She punched all the information into her computer. I asked her where he was. Her answer nearly floored me.

It seems that in 1971, federal legislation had been passed in the wake of a credit scam. Credit reporting and collection agencies had overstepped their bounds and were invading the privacy of many consumers. The Privacy Act of 1971 was passed allowing information to be released only with the consent of the individual. I was informed she could not release the information of my father's whereabouts. She said that a letter would be sent to my father asking for permission to release the information, and that I would have to wait for an answer until he replied. Blocked again!

My second plan was to return to the phone and call as many people as I could in the Memphis area, hoping that I would strike the chord that would give me the information I sought. All I received was a silent thank-you from Wall Street where my long distance carrier's stock was soaring.

At this time I would like to thank Mary Ann Bryant, Delores Brown and Rosalie Owens (Scola), all supervisors with South Central Bell. It was these wonderful women who kept my spirits afloat and who saved me from paying a bill of several thousand dollars instead of the several hundred I did pay.

When my juvenile record finally arrived, I learned that Scola was the married name of my mother's sister. As it turned out, Rosalie Owens (Scola) was my cousin, one of Stella's children. Of the three supervisors, she had been the most helpful. Later, I learned that when I told her the details of the family I was looking for, she wondered if we were related. She had a sister whose name was the same as my mother's, Kathleen Rheba. Rosie was prevented from disclosing this fact because the phone company was monitoring the conversations of all employees, including the supervisors. Her revelation would have gotten her in a lot of trouble. Once I learned the maiden name of my mother, I began looking for phone numbers of Scola family members. The number I found was that of Uncle Tony Scola.

I had already contacted Cheri Matthews at the Modesto Bee. We had been collaborating on a story for three weeks. Cheri was not just another reporter with a pretty face and figure. She had been awarded the California Newspaper Publishers Association Award for best feature writing, the previous year. When I called Cheri on the 28th of February with the news, she instructed me to come down to the Bee Building immediately. She would listen in and take notes while I made the call from a conference room. After my conversation with Uncle Tony had ended, Cheri entered the room with a ball of tissue wadded up in her hand. Her eyes were as red as cherries in June. I chuckled to myself and asked her, "What's your problem?" We both laughed. "What's all that on the table?" Cheri shot back at me. I hadn't noticed the small pool of teardrops shimmering in the glow of the florescent lights. We laughed again.

I informed Cheri of my need to go home to freshen up before the pictures were shot. She seemed truly alarmed. I felt she was afraid I was going to run to the airport and jump on the next plane to Memphis. The thought never crossed my mind.

I returned at the appointed time and met the staff photographer, Ted Benson. Ted and I had gone to Davis High together, where he worked on the school newspaper and yearbook. Ted and Cheri had worked together for many years. The pictures were taken and we settled into a pleasant conversation with Ted telling us about his family. After he left, Cheri said here she had worked with Ted all those years and never heard his story before!

This is an illustration of one of the most pleasant transformations in my life. Finding my family had immediately affected my attitude toward my life and the people in it. People now open up their personal lives to me where they never could before.

I was in Memphis when the story came out. Cheri sent me a copy. I talked to a reporter in Memphis, but the Memphis Commercial Appeal refused to put my story in their paper. Marylin, the reporter I talked to, advised me that so many reunions had recently happened that it wasn't worth their time. I suppose murderers and crooks make for greater sensationalism and sell more papers. Too bad!

In any case, I had marched around the walls of the bureaucracy blowing my horn at intervals and the wall came tumbling down. All that remained was to enter the city to claim my birth right.

CHAPTER FOURTEEN
The Journey Home

I left Modesto, California, on Sunday morning, March 8, 1992. East to Memphis was my destination and my destiny. My heart fluttered like that of a little child getting himself ready to leave for school for the first time. Placing all of my love and trust in the hands of Him who had protected me all my life, I recalled the story of Moses wandering in the desert. The terrible struggles I had endured and the bitter anger that had grown inside of me were tempered by my knowledge that I could not be here experiencing this triumph and weeping these tears of joy had I not wept the bitter tears of my life.

A person could not want a finer friend than Karen Johnson who drove me to the train depot in Riverbank, California. The train station I was leaving from had always been important to me. I had been picking up and dropping off my son, Andrew, at this station for several years. I did this to avoid contact with his mom because we always argued. This is not good for Andrew. The train station was more important now than it had ever been. It had always been my major link to Andrew. Now it was an umbilical cord stretching across the continent to my biological family back east.

Norma and Martha, the two lady ticket attendants, were smiling radiantly when I walked in. I had gotten to know them over the years of chauffeuring Andrew back and forth to the station for his visits with me. My ticket was waiting for me having already been prepaid by Ollie and Rosalie Owens, my cousins on Mom's side. Rosie's mother, Aunt Stella, was the one who wished to adopt me and was refused by the Juvenile Court. They had also begun a search for Sis and me while I was conducting my search for them. I felt humble and grateful that they had done this for me.

Andrew had always had the advantage over me in knowing what it was like to travel by train. Now I would find out why he enjoyed so much traveling this way. I had a hunch it would be exciting.

Over the years I have collected beautiful little German-made figurines called Hummels. One of my favorite figurines in my collection is called the "Merry Wanderer." That was I, the little boy packed and waiting for the train.

Thoughts of my daughter, Jennifer, rippled across the waters of my mind. She lives in Sacramento, California. I guessed she was not even out of bed yet.

The train steamed in from the south. Only a few passengers were taking the ride on this day. I handed Karen my camera. She expertly shot the cus-

tomary pictures as the baggage was being stowed.
Last minute hugs and kisses left a lasting memory in
my heart. The adrenaline was rushing through me
like a locomotive with no tracks. Tears oozed from
the corners of my eyes. The flavor of those bitter-
sweet moments stills graces my lips.

Karen's farewell hugs and kisses were given
with an unusual amount of energy, especially the kiss.
I have had many over the years, from a small army
of beautiful women. Karen's kiss was special and
more moving than all of them put together. It left me
wishing she had kissed me like that long before I
boarded the train. Karen's smile was like a cat that
has just eaten a canary. She knew she was safe giving me that kiss since I would soon be speeding away
on an adventure she would have loved to have been
on. But, had she gone with me, I wouldn't have the
memory of that special kiss to carry with me always.

As the train slowly chugged out of the station,
I noticed the day was a mixture of broken clouds
and sunshine. I stared out the big windows as Karen,
Norma and Martha slowly sank out of sight. For just
an instant, my body quaked with fear. The familiar
was fading into the distance. My immediate past, the
good and the bad, was shrinking from sight as I
sought to make an even stronger connection between
my distant past and my future. And how about that
future? Would my family receive me with love, or

would they push me away? I reminded myself of my
resolve not to set myself up for another fall. In my
mind, I went over the goals I had set for myself. I
was halfway through them when the conductor came
down the aisle punching tickets.

The conductor, I learned in subsequent days,
is in charge of the train. I had always thought that
the engineer was in charge. As he punched my ticket,
I couldn't help but tell him I was going home to meet
my family for the first time in my life. One contact
led to another. Before I knew it, several passengers
were involved in the conversation. All were wishing
me the best. I actually believed in people again.

As the train picked up speed, the countryside
flew by. We were headed north to Stockton. This was
the same scenery my son had watched on his train
travels. It made me feel a little closer to him, yet I
still puzzled over the obvious pleasure he showed
for his rides on the train.

The first clue was found in the club car. This
place is a child's delight, stuffed with candy, soda,
pizza slices and friendly attendants who fawn over
little children. There were also souvenirs, cakes and
pies. The prices seemed high, but it was expected.
For Andrew, who is given money and is lucky to be
young and not have to work yet, prices mean nothing. Some day the cookie jar will dry up, and he will
have to work for his money, but, until then, he will

be in heaven whenever he boards the train.

This train ride, my first ever, whisked me away on an adventure of the type only a man like Jules Vern could think up. Excitement and intrigue lurked around every corner. My attention was constantly divided between the scenery, the people in the car and the thoughts in my mind.

At Martinez, California, we disembarked. Martinez is a small city situated on the waterfront near San Francisco. Intimidating, like a giant dinosaur, the skeleton of the Martinez Bridge rose several hundred feet. Before we boarded the double-decker, "California Zephyr", a layover of a couple of hours had to be endured. Zephyr, the wind, would take me across this great country to Chicago where another train would be waiting. The Zephyr arrived at last and the winds of time wrapped me safely in her bosom knowing what a special child she was accompanying.

How many times have I had to stop to wait for a train to cross the road? On this trip I had the fun of being the one waited on. At one point in my adventure, our train stopped in the middle of a road. I can recall peering through my car window at the anonymous faces occupying the cars parked at the crossing. I wondered where this person or that person was from and where they were traveling. Were they also on their way home after forty some years? I figured the chances were very slim. I thought of all the souls who were heading home thanks to Denny Glad and all of the people in the world like her.

I waved at the passengers in the cars, and they waved back.

I made many acquaintances on this trip. Some of them even gave me their names and addresses. They told me to drop them a line when I had a chance.

"Drop a line" is an interesting cliché all of us have heard frequently over the years. I viewed a Public Broadcasting System program on the subject of early mail delivery from many years ago. Two tall wood poles were erected at specific locations around the country. Stretched between the two poles was a cable. Attached to the cable, approximately thirty feet overhead, was the local mail pouch. A plane would fly directly over the apparatus with a line hanging down attached to a hook that would snag the mail pouch. The plane would then drop the mail pouch destined for that area. Hence we get the cliché, "drop a line."

I also gave my fellow passengers my address. Nothing has ever come of those addresses. Man is an unusual creature. He will ask for things that he has no intention of using. And life goes on.

Our next stop was Davis, California followed by Roseville. Before us lay the formidable Sierras. I had driven across them countless times. Driving never truly enables one to enjoy their beauty. The Zephyr allowed me to kick back and enjoy the scenery.

A party of gamblers boarded in Roseville. Reno was their destination. They were all wound up with excitement and ready to hit the tables where each one expected to win a fortune but would probably lose everything except the holes in their souls.

I hadn't been taking many pictures up to this point, but that was to change quickly. My goal at the start of my adventure was to keep a picture log. Each time I took a picture, I was going to jot down a few notes about it. This lasted halfway across the Sierras. There was too much going on. If I were busy writing notes, I would miss out on some of the best pictures of my life. The rational mind is such a wonderful contraption. It invents methods of getting done what we want to do, then, when we tire of our task, it invents a rationale for abandoning it.

The California Zephyr is a double-decker train, government subsidized and operated by Amtrak. The car I was on was ahead of the dining car, the dome car and the club car. The dome car was furnished with benches and bucket seats. What set it apart from the regular cars was the positioning of the seats: they faced the windows on both sides. I took many pictures from that car.

Below the dome car was the club car. I spent a

great deal of time down there. The back half of the club car was for smoking. What a laugh! The whole car was filled with smoke.

I bought myself travelers' coffee cup that said "Ski Amtrak". One of the train attendants told me that the purchase of this cup entitled me to free refills. It was one of the smartest purchases I made on my odyssey. I drank out of the same cup all the way across America. This cup will be in my cupboard a long time to remind me of my trip.

This was such a romantic period in my life, and there was no girlfriend to share it with. Realizing that I did not need a partner present to experience feelings of romance while riding the steel horse to my beginnings was delicious. I settled in to watch the two most interesting things before me, the scenery and the people. The peoples' actions and faces spoke volumes to me. Their antics provided me with constant amusement while the stunningly beautiful scenery presented itself to my camera lens.

About halfway through the Sierras, I needed to get some more film for my camera. I had stored my briefcase and a suitcase stuffed with food above my passenger seat. My two suitcases of clothing were sent straight through to Chicago. When I opened my briefcase, an envelope greeted my eyes that I didn't remember packing. Inside was a card from Karen. She had enclosed some money and wrote on the card,

"Have a nice dinner on me." I actually had a couple
of good dinners on her. I was so proud she had done
this. She must have put the card in my briefcase back
in Riverbank while I was busy with the ticket attendants. She also enclosed a chocolate bar, one of the
kind kids' sell at school for fund-raisers.

It being only March, the peaks of the Sierras
were covered with snow. We were climbing Donner
Summit, the scene of a terrible tragedy that happened
when the West was young. Outside the train, the tem-
perature was substantially colder. Though my flesh
was warm, the cold outside seeped into my spirit.
What a tragedy it would be if an avalanche came
tumbling down on the train burying my lifelong
dream under tons of snow and ice!

By the time we pulled into Reno, Nevada, the
gamblers had drunk enough courage to challenge the
casinos. The casinos were ready. I've always thought
the casinos are sneaky. First they give a gambler a
couple of free drinks to loosen up his judgment, then
they fleece the poor sucker who is thinking how nice
they are for giving him free drinks.

Free drinks cost me dearly in the past. No one
was around to teach me this fact of life, but I sure as
hell plan to teach Andrew so he doesn't learn the
hard way. God! I lost a lot in life by not having loving parents.

We had a two-hour layover in Reno. I stayed

near the train. I had already lost my share at the gambling tables. Gambling, like drinking, is an addiction I can ill afford. I had worked no more than a few blocks from the train station, several years earlier. Gambling and drinking drove me involuntarily from my job. I thought, "How ironic for me to finally be heading home and passing through some of the places where I spent many of my most irresponsible years."

At each stop, the wait seemed too long. I had taken the train to savor this ride home, but impatience was already making me squirm in my seat. Darkness settled in for the night. The only things visible were the lights of homes and businesses and the cars along the roads and freeways. As long as the train ran along a freeway, the engineer was required to not exceed a particular speed limit. I noticed, however, that as soon as the headlights of the cars on the highway disappeared, the train roared down the track much faster.

We crossed the Great Salt Lake. I had been through this area eleven years before and had not lost any sleep not seeing it again. As a young boy I had been interested in reading about the land speed records being set here in Bonneville. Now the salt flats were just that: flat and dark. My interest turned to the passengers in my car.

When the Zephyr slid into Salt Lake City,

Utah, the station was deserted. On our way out of town, we passed the Mormon Tabernacle.

As we came close to each stop along the way, we were notified that the train's restrooms were off limits. I learned from one of the train attendants that when we used the restroom, the toilets emptied directly onto the tracks. We were able to resume using them again, when we were outside the city limits. No dumping within city limits!

One of the interesting rituals of crossing America by train is the constant changing of the guard. The trip to Memphis took three hours short of four days to complete. By the time I arrived there, I had recited the story of finding my family so many times that I was starting to sound like a recording. Of course, there were many people on the train that I never met. Most of those I did meet were smokers. Occasionally a passenger would come into the club car with a brown paper bag. The bag concealed the bottle of booze from which they were drinking. If I were still drinking, I would be pulling the same trick.

The passengers were not the only people boarding and leaving the train. Amtrak attendants were changed at various stations. Some of them were friendly and some weren't. The friendly attendants were fun to talk to. They were full of information that only they could have, due to the nature of their jobs. Each one of them said that the hardest part of the job is dealing with dysfunctional passengers. At one of the stops, a passenger had to be picked up by a waiting ambulance. It happened that he suffered an epileptic seizure while on the train. Several others were asked to disembark for smoking pot in the rest rooms and others for being drunk.

The second day of my adventure home found us streaking across Utah and Colorado. As I said before, I took the train to enjoy the anticipation of meeting my family. In a few days, I would experience the most wonderful climax of my life. And I would have done it my way. I could have been in Memphis in three hours by plane. What fun would that have been? I wouldn't have been able to say I had crossed the Rocky Mountains in the dead of winter. I wouldn't have met the people I met nor enjoyed the scenery I was to see on this trip. What could I tell my grandchildren about my trip if it had taken only three hours? Most importantly, I wanted to enjoy my final days in Hell.

There were few stops in Utah. However, the rock formations were quite impressive. I have seen many pictures of the unusual rock formations and am always fascinated by those striking shapes splashed onto canvas earth by an invisible hand. As we passed them by, I tried to imagine how rugged the travelers were who had journeyed westward in pursuit of hopes and dreams in a new land.

We began our climb into Colorado, a state I had flown into often during my stint in the Air Force Reserves. The reason for my excursions to Colorado was for Administrative Assistance visits to our subordinate units in Denver and Colorado Springs. I learned early in life to enjoy the scenery and beauty of this great country whenever the opportunity presents itself. Colorado has always been one of my favorite sights to see. Now I was seeing the state by train.

The climb up the west face of the Rockies was slow at best. The passengers were not privy to the information about the weather front on the east side of those magnificent mountains. A snowstorm had just dumped twenty inches of fresh powder on the Denver area. The delay set us back four hours. Much of the beauty we were primed to enjoy was hidden from us by the dark of night.

We snaked through approximately fifty tunnels while traversing the young mountain range of America. One tunnel was eleven miles long. While chugging through that tunnel, I wondered why those Hollywood film people never based a disaster movie on a train trapped inside a mountain tunnel by an avalanche. On an impulse, I asked one of the attendants how deep the snow could pile up before the train would have to stop. His reply was four feet. I was growing tired of canned Spam and fruit cocktail, the provisions stuffed into my suitcase to help me save money on my eats, so I decided to treat myself to a dinner in the dining car, complements of Karen.

The tables were set nicely with silver, linen, glassware and flowers. If there hadn't been a window framing the ever-changing landscape, I would have thought I was back home in a nice little restaurant. The setting was quite elegant. While dining on a roasted half-chicken, I could see herds of deer grazing in the lengthening shadows along the Colorado River. I had seen this kind of beauty before only on postcards. What a lucky man I was! The four-day train ride was worth just this one moment. And I still had my family to meet.

Although we lost four hours of daylight going through the Rockies, the sight of Denver as we left the mountains was beautiful. As far as I could see, there were millions of twinkling lights. The descent into Denver took almost as much time as the climb up the west face. When the train made the station, snow was piled everywhere.

A sweet lady who had been accompanying her wheelchair-bound father needed help. Managing her elderly father and all the luggage they were carrying was proving too much for her. A couple of other passengers and myself helped her disembark. She was a strong woman emotionally. I had met her when we left Riverbank. She lived across the street from the high school I had graduated from. All too often I have seen people turn their backs on their parents when the parents needed help in their old age. Well, this kind lady would never be accused of "granny dropping." I was sure of that.

I now noticed that the small train that had left Martinez had grown considerably. By the time we reached Denver, the number of cars had increased to fourteen. At times, depending on the sweep of curve in the track we were following, the front part of the train would disappear. It was like watching a snake slither back and forth.

My trip was undoubtedly, austere. I would have loved to have had a sleeper car, but they were $90 more per day. I couldn't afford that. My body ached to stretch out for some sleep. The passengers' seats did recline and were comfortable to sit in, but to sleep was difficult. I noticed that many of the passengers had empty seats adjoining theirs, so they would use both seats as small beds. I tried to do likewise, but soon realized being a large man had its drawbacks.

We stopped in Denver for a brief layover. The lost time had to be made up, so off we flew. Thoughts of a mother I never would meet flooded my mind.

I was listening to Richard Marx singing his best selling song, "Right Here Waiting." The song touched my heart. For the first time, I felt the spirit of my mother touching me. I knew from that point on that Mom was accompanying me on my journey home. Again the tears flowed, and I vowed to do the best I could with the rest of my life. In my mind, I could hear her speaking to me. Her words were comforting. Since then she has been with me in my daily life. All I have to do is think of her, and I can feel her presence.

I don't ever plan on disgracing my mother's love. This love is a feeling I have never known before. It made me think how proud my mother would have been of me for overcoming all the pain and other obstacles I have triumphed over. She would have been proud of herself for making the correct decision in giving Sis and me up for adoption. She was right. She tried to keep us, but when she couldn't do that any longer, she made the right choice. True, we did experience much hardship, but it made us stronger individuals. People have to be strong to survive. Not enough is said about the strength of the average working man and woman. These people have to face the daily grind, balance on a tight wire between enough and not enough and have the courage to get up to face each day knowing ahead of time of the struggle each day will bring. Instead, the wealthy and notorious receive the majority of the headlines as the commoner trudges along. You will never see a headline about a father who dug out the family's sewer line after working a ten-hour day so that the money could be saved for the children's Christmas. You will never see a headline about a mother washing clothes out by hand after a hard day of labor, because the washer is broken and the family cannot afford to fix it, or to go to the Laundromat.

Love is a continuum, traveling constantly through the avenues of space and time from one spirit to another. I felt that spirit constantly on my journey home.

It is four a.m. The light of my desk lamp is illuminating the face of my sleeping ten-year-old son. So peacefully he sleeps, while Dad writes this autobiography. He is such a beautiful little man growing up with hardships inherent in a split family. He is resilient, as all children are. He will make it. His chances are greater than were mine. I pray to God to protect this fine child of His. At times it is difficult for me to appreciate how wonderful a gift from God he is. I am moved that I have been so blessed. One day he and Jennifer will read their dad's autobiography and realize how special they are.

Of course, all that changes when the little man opens his eyes and the lights in his head switch on. Moments like these are priceless. The real work starts when they wake up. Here I am at mid-life, looking at my surroundings which aren't really all that bad, thinking this little sleeping vessel will carry into the coming years the embodiment of mankind. I work to teach him the right things in life. I pray for him and his future. There may be times when he doesn't have two pennies to rub together, but I will make sure he knows how to remedy the problem. He may find himself in other situations that all the money in the world will not solve. I will try to give him the tools to deal with this part of life as well.

My name in Greek means, "one who has his hands in the dirt." The farmer continues from generation to generation to pass on the truest values of life. He has learned that his life and the lives of his children, and his grandchildren, depend on Mother Earth. Treat her well and she will treat you well. In Nebraska and Iowa, the land is flat and the people simple and great. They are mostly farmers who are hard working and closer to nature than many of the rest of us are. One of my favorite bumper stickers is the one that reads, "Don't complain about farmers with your mouth full."

When we screeched to a halt in Lincoln, Nebraska, I remembered reading about a football coach in this state. His name was Bob Devaney. Old Bob was a pretty good coach, and his players liked him. They played well for him and were always on the hunt for a national championship. I had forgotten about him for twenty years. Our train glided slowly past the stadium named after him. It was good that I recalled who Bob Devaney was. He didn't set out in life to have a football stadium named after him. He set out to do the best job he could by coaching young men.

The day was splendidly clear and exhilarating when the train crossed the Missouri River into Illinois. A young man around thirty shuffled into the club car. He was fascinating and very handsome. He was also artistic. His passion for life was only excelled by his passion for beer. He possessed several harmonicas of different shapes and sizes. He told me he had been a driver of funeral hearses. I too would probably drink a lot, if I had that kind of job. I used to drink for lesser reasons.

Evidently, he was on a budget smaller than mine was. Pay as you go travel, they call it. He whipped out his harmonicas and puffed out one lively tune after another. The club car resounded with his energy. People would make requests, and he would oblige. In return, some of the passengers bought him beer. Within half an hour, he had earned five bottles, four of which sat unopened on the seat beside him. I gave him an admiring glance, and he smiled back. He was brilliant, and he knew it.

Train themes in movies are well known: Dr. Zhivago, Bridge over the River Kwai, Silver Streak, etc. Dr. Zhivago is my favorite. I saw this classic when I was younger with a special girl who eventually accepted my proposal for marriage. In one of the scenes from the movie, a Russian train is racing east across the frozen tundra of Siberia accompanied by "Laura's Theme." Somehow, this stranger and his music reminded me of this melodic song. The stranger was excellent at playing the blues. His harmonica cried real tears. The snow blew by our windows glistening in the daylight as the man's music poured from his soul. Good blues makes one think of suffering. My thoughts turned to Mom and how she must have suffered while agonizing over the decision she had to make and live with the rest of her brief life.

Illinois means Chicago and Chicago meant action. We arrived in Chicago for a short layover. The sight of the skyline punctuated by the Sears Tower, the tallest building in the world, grabbed me. Now I was in the city of Elliott Ness and Frank Nitty of the Untouchables. Chicago lived up to its nickname, The Windy City, on this day. In addition to wind, there was snow driven onto the frozen landscape.

The icy wind, cutting through clothing and flesh, to chill the marrow, made me think of how cold life had been for me. And I had nearly allowed that cold to chill my spirit and dump my body by the wayside where it would be buried in the snow. It could have been different. The courts could have al-

lowed the Scolas to adopt Sis and me. Mom might
still be in the picture if Judge Kelley had allowed
that to happen. She and I would have had the opportunity to know each other. Sis and I would have had
a family who wanted both of us. "What ifs" are fine
for speculation, but we have to live with what is.
Now it was my duty to present myself to my lost
family. I was uncertain of the welcome I would be
receiving. I was not sure they would like me. As my
journey neared its end, I could only hold the mixture
of emotions in check by reminding myself of my
goals and their importance.

As we backed into the station in Chicago, I
noticed burning smudge pots at different intervals.
It confused me at first. I thought the tracks were on
fire. I was about to tell one of the attendants when
the thought occurred to me that the fires were inten-
tional. Upon closer inspection, it was revealed the
fires were burning next to the switches for the tracks.
The purpose was to keep the switches from freezing
shut. Man can be extremely ingenious.

My bags with all my clothes in them had to be
picked up since they were sent straight through to
Chicago. When this task was accomplished, I had a
chance to explore Union Station. There was no time
for anything else. The station was cavernous. I had
never seen such a high ceiling. I felt like a dwarf. I
broke out my Sure Shot and snapped pictures from

different perspectives. I had to capture the immensity of this building, and I succeeded.

Too soon the time was at hand to board the final train for Memphis. This train had a great deal of emotion associated with it. I had learned that my mother had died in Chicago. Mom was forty-two years old when she died of cirrhosis of the liver, a condition compounded many years earlier when she was forced to give my sister and me up for adoption. She drank herself to death grieving over us. I learned this from the family. She had been married for sixteen years to a black man named Jimmy Campbell. As far as anyone knows, she had no more children. Chicago had been one of Mom's playgrounds. I learned upon my arrival in Memphis that Aunt Stella, my mother's older sister, went to Chicago to bring Mom's remains back to Memphis. Mr. Campbell was not going to allow Stella to do this, but acquiesced upon Stella's insistence. In return, he kept all of Mom's personal belongings. I would have liked to have met with Mr. Campbell to talk with him concerning Mom, but he passed away a few years ago. Some day I hope to find Mr. Campbell's family. I have the information to do so. When Mr. Campbell died a few years ago, in Chicago, he took with him the memories of my mother's final days.

The train was once again my home for the next twelve hours. This train was a single level train like the one from Riverbank to Martinez. It was crowded and uncomfortable. Again, I occupied the club car. It was dark by this time, and the club car rocked with the sound of revelers. The way one couple was behaving, I was sure they were going to have sex on the floor. They were both drunk beyond sensibility. Intertwined, they writhed together on the floor at the feet of a crowd of indifferent people.

I had been warned by fellow travelers to be careful of the prostitutes. They were permanent fixtures on this train. As I sat in the club car, I spotted one of them. She was an attractive woman with silky smooth ebony skin. Her eyes kept meeting mine, and I felt a compulsion to attend to her. In the old days when I was drunk much of the time, and had the money, I might have been persuaded. But I am sober and much more cautious now. I turned to peer out the window and was met with her reflection. She was still staring at me. After a bit, I fell asleep. When I awoke, she was gone, but the memory was mine.

Many years ago, a young pop singer named Arlo Gutherie Jr. scored a number one hit on the charts. It has always been one of my favorite songs. The name of the song was "The City of New Orleans." It was a ballad about a train. The significance had been lost on me then, but now I understood what Gutherie was singing about. The "City of New Orleans," was a train that had for years carried travelers north and south from Chicago to New Orleans. Unknowingly, I had been listening all this time to a song about a train that was my mother's hearse.

The train was rocketing down the track at a faster rate. I could tell by the change in the pace of the clickity-clack of the wheels on the rails. Lights were zipping by. I became alarmed at the rate of speed we were traveling. I have always had a high anxiety level. Impending doom has been my constant companion. The doomsayer in my brain was now shaking his head and muttering how deeply tragic it would be if this sucker derails, and I get splattered all over the tracks just a few miles from my destination and my family. He always comes up with his quick, suffering wit to remind me I might die at any moment. I now understand why he does this. The doomsayer's hair-raising horoscopes of my future give me renewed energy to fight against anything that might be in my way. Whether it is abusive parents or religious dogma, he is always there spurring me on with his horror stories.

We were to make Memphis by six a.m. At five a.m., while every one else was sleeping, I began to prepare myself for the moment of a lifetime. I was about to be reborn. My anticipation and nervousness were incredible.

The train had no shower, but it did have wash basins. I stripped to the waist and shaved. I couldn't

believe this was happening. My good intentions of
wearing a suit, so my family would see a handsome
well-dressed man, were crushed by the bulldozer
called reality. I realized that the suit would be nice,
but was impractical. It would also have been phony.
I never wear suits except to weddings or funerals. I
wanted the family to see the real me.

Somehow I managed to wash my hair in the
small sink. I blow-dried my hair and changed into
some fresh clothes. All was ready with a half-hour
to spare.

I walked back to the club car for another cancer stick. Karen had loaned me her Walkman radio
for companionship on the adventure. I believe she
would have enjoyed being there for that family reunion. Family is important in her life, as it should be
for all of us. Though Karen was not there physically,
I carried her in my heart along with the goodness of
all those who believe in love.

I slipped the headset on and tuned in to a new
station. The disc jockey announced that the tempera-
ture was thirty-six degrees in Memphis. We passed a
sign advertising, of all places, "The Brass Rail." I
wondered if it could be the same "Brass Rail", the
scene of a nasty brawl forty-two years before which
had affected my life. I toyed with the idea of investi-
gating. My final conclusion was that there was nothing there for me. I was wrong to think this.

The next song on the radio was Johnny River's "Long Distance Information Give Me Memphis Tennessee." How appropriate to be hearing this song as we squeaked to a stop at the station in Memphis, my home and birthplace.

Daylight was breaking over the river city. Memphis, an Egyptian word meaning city by the river, was before me now, and the past four sleepless nights were but a memory. The city seemed different from the last time I was here. It was different. Now I had found my family. Within a few minutes, I would be embracing them and making a lifelong dream come true. Would they accept me and want to know me? Would they be as nervous and unsure as I was, at the moment we touched for the first time in forty years? Rays of golden sunlight streamed down on the city as I awaited the answers to my questions.

CHAPTER FIFTEEN
Lazarus

On that cold, clear morning I stepped from the train in Memphis, exhausted from four days of traveling with only eight hours of fitful sleep. Disoriented and worried that my adrenaline would run out before my task would be completed, I tried to remain the merry wanderer, but I felt more like I had just recrossed the River Jordan. In the meantime, the city was coming alive.

My fears clouded my mind as my warm breath veiled the crisp air in front of me. I lugged my travel cases across the tarmac to a long staircase seeming to descend into the bowels of Hell. It was then, along with my other fears, I realized I did not know much about the physical characteristics of the relatives I was to meet. A brief comment my cousin Rosalie had made concerning the large size of her son Mark came to mind.

With only this shred of information to comfort me, I entered the station where several people were milling around. My stomach tightened as I began searching the crowd for the eyes that were assuredly searching for me. I peered right into the eyes of Mark, Rosalie's son. Indeed, he was a large young man. Rosalie and her husband, Ollie, were next to Mark. I can tell you that between the four of us, there weren't too many meals missed. Other than our portly bearing, the only resemblance was in the eyes.

All of our eyes filled with tears as we rushed together to experience the closeness of a few healthy hugs. My legs turned to rubber, but was there anyone else from the family there to greet me? I wanted more family. I was like a child who has opened his last Christmas present and, before examining what he has already opened, he searches through the ripped wrapping papers, bows and ribbons for one he might have missed. In the end, I had to be satisfied with the three wonderful presents there.

Mark's reaction was one of curiosity. Being only twenty-one and a generation removed, he exhibited very little emotion. When he did, it was appropriate. He was happy for me, but he was also happy for his mother. I think that says a lot about this fine young man.

Ollie was such a gentleman. After properly greeting me, he retrieved my luggage while Rosalie and I hugged and cried. Ollie then gently ushered us into the parking lot where a late model Volvo awaited us. Mark and Ollie took the front seat leaving the back to Rosalie and me. I was right where I wanted to be. With my cousin close, I was able to peer at the sights of Memphis between the shoulders of the two large men in the front of me.

As we drove through the streets of Memphis,

the ghosts of years past rose up to line the sidewalks. I was feeling the presence of my mother again, and Aunt Stella, who had also passed away, was there as well. My own spirit, so long in the realm of the dead, also began to rise up.

The lost son was now returned. The prayers my mother must have made were now being answered. I felt she would be so proud. She had given birth to a truly remarkable son, not because I say so, but because the story of his life says it.

I shared these thoughts with Rosalile. She said she also felt Mother's presence. We were both grateful at the magic in this moment. I could feel the changes already being wrought in my life. The windows to my soul were opening. Sunlight and fresh air were streaming in. My attitudes would never be the same. I would never again feel unaccountable for my behavior. With my mother's spirit watching me, I would have to behave myself to keep from embarrassing her or her memory.

The four of us stopped for breakfast. Rosalie probably realized I would appreciate a good hot meal after being on the road for four days. A beautiful little boy and his mother appeared at the table. The child was Rosie's grandson, Christopher. I could see generations of my family in Christopher's eyes. One day he will be a handsome, intelligent adult. While that is happening, for the first time, I will be able to observe the growth of my family.

As small talk was exchanged, the miracle of this event began to strain my emotions. A wall of mankind's stupidity had separated my family and me. What we were experiencing wasn't supposed to happen. I should have gone to my grave never having met these wonderful people.

I asked Rosie if, during the forty years since I had vanished from the family's presence, anyone had thought I had died. Yes, some had been concerned that I had died. In a sense, I was like Lazarus. At the age of twenty-three days, I entered the, "Tomb of Doom." My entry into TCHS was the beginning of a journey through Hell. Now I was sitting quietly eating and visiting with my family. The grace of God had raised me up to again experience the joys of life.

We arrived at Rosie and Ollie's home. It is an attractive home of brick with a beauty that radiates from within. The physical structure was aesthetically pleasing to my eyes, and I experienced gladness in my heart that I had at last come home.

As I unpacked, my weariness caught up with me. Ollie and Rosie had set me at ease. Tonight, I would be able to relax into a deep, renewing sleep and prepare myself for the events to come.

CHAPTER SIXTEEN
A Family Album

Late in the afternoon, I was led into the formal dining area. Rosie knows how to decorate a home exquisitely. In this lovely room where Rosie's silver and china were on display, I was shown the family pictures.

While I stayed with Rosie and Ollie, I was treated like a king. Everyone was not only kind to me, but they waited on me hand and foot. Ollie is a wonderful cook and makes especially good meatballs. He was in the kitchen at the time I was viewing the family album, fixing supper to delight us all.

The first picture of Mom was placed before me. I couldn't believe my eyes! Uncle Tony had told me that Mom was one of the most beautiful women in Memphis. At the time, I felt he had said that to make me feel good after years of not knowing. He had not exaggerated one bit.

Mom was not only beautiful, but, unexpectedly, she looked exactly like my sister Kathy. I began to feel lightheaded as the color drained from my face. There was no mistaking the resemblance of Sis and Mom. Rosie, seeing my tears, began to cry as well.

When I returned to Modesto, my first stop was at Jack's On D, the restaurant-lounge where Kathy is employed as a bartender. She was working at the time, and several patrons were seated at the bar. I arrived with my hands full of pictures and began showing them around and asking if they knew whom the person was in the pictures. No one knew I had just returned from Memphis. Every one agreed that the person in the pictures was Kathy.

Kathy, always the big sister, likes to pretend she isn't listening or watching little brother. However, her curiosity got the best of her this time. She sidled down the bar to see what her little brother was up to. When I handed her the pictures, she was speechless for the first time I can remember. I watched her like Rosie had watched me. The expression of shock and disbelief on her face told the story.

Rosie and I viewed several more pictures before she placed a snap shot of a very handsome man in front of me. "That is your father," she said. Again I was shocked. Seeing this picture of my father removed the last vestige of my lost identity.

When a person knows their parents, they are able to look to them for their identity. They can see where they came from. They can make judgments about themselves and how they look based on the mirror provided by the physical presence of parents. A child deprived of this opportunity suffers much anguish in their lives not knowing where they came from.

Because I had no psychological bonding with
my parents, I was able to evaluate their physical ap-
pearances objectively. There could be no mistaking
the physical attraction they saw in each other. My
estimation of how their relationship started could be
aptly described by my favorite Mel Brooks movie,
"Lust in the Dust".

Our joy was to be interrupted by a trip to Mothers grave. Rosie, Mark and little Christopher, Rosie's
adorable grandson, and I piled into the car. On the
ride to the cemetery, I couldn't help but remember
one of the more moving scenes from the Sixty Minutes episode I had viewed with my friend Karen. The
sight of a fellow scandal survivor, a strong and courageous woman about the same age as myself, kneel-
ing next to the grave of her mother had torn at my
heartstrings. Remember that I vowed I would not
consider my mother dead until I knelt at her graveside
as this woman had. Soon, I would be reenacting this
scene. So many feelings were stirring inside me I
found it difficult to cope with them all.

We paid our respects to Aunt Stella first before going on to Mother's grave. It seemed to take
forever to find it. Rosie told me how Aunt Stella took
care of the funeral arrangements. I thought again of
how Aunt Stella had brought Mom's remains home
from Chicago. Mom died in 1967 when I was

graduating from high school. Her life ended with the family at the age of forty-two, the same age my life with the family began. And the train they call the City of New Orleans brought us both home.

Standing there at Mom's grave, with a few clouds plying the cold air above us, I was at a loss for words. I tried to look through the ground to see her remains buried six feet below. All I could see was the tear-smeared sod covering her, but I began to feel her presence as I had on several occasions during my trip. I knelt down and touched the ground with my hand while her spirit touched my heart. Yes, Mom was dead, but despite my never knowing her when she was alive, her spirit would live on in my heart forever. All of us began to cry again.

I was left alone with Mom. The search for her was now complete. The tears of sadness I had cried all my life were now turned to tears of true joy. I would never be the same. All that now remained to complete the circle was for me to find Dad.

Rosie and the others returned. There were puzzled expressions on their faces. When I inquired about their puzzlement, I was told that Rosie had lost a little brother at a young age, less than two years. His name was Johnny. Rosie had been trying to find his grave, but had met with little success until she remembered Johnny was buried at Mom's feet so they would have each other in eternal peace. This way

Mom did have a little boy with her for eternity.

While we were there, we visited Grandpa Kirk's grave. The story of Mom's father is an interesting one. Grandpa Charlie Kirk (Castillion and Cherokee Indian) was a World War I veteran. He had been a muleskinner during the war. He drove ammo wagons, cracking the whip with precision near the ears of the mules to prod them on. He drank too much whiskey, and it made him go crazy. Being half Cherokee, he had the same problem with alcohol other native Americans have had since being introduced to the white man's firewater.

The stories I have been privy to concerning Grandpa Charlie's behavior while intoxicated are hilarious and sad at the same time. However, a normal and sober spouse is not going to tolerate a drunkard for very long. My second wife, Nancy, would be quick to agree, God love her. Grandma Hessie Kirk (Haynes), one of ten children and my Great Aunt Lessie's Twin, of Irish descent, reacted with Grandpa Charlie the same way Nancy reacted with me, she left him.

Charlie and Hessie had three children, Charlie, Stella, and Kathleen, my mom. Once Charlie's drinking destroyed the marriage, Hessie turned for comfort to John Hall, a sharecropper from Arkansas. When Charlie found out about the alliance between the two, he horsewhipped John Hall and told them if he ever saw either one of them in Memphis again, he would kill them.

Hessie and John quickly moved away leaving Charlie with three children. Charlie Jr. was able to fend for himself. Stella got married. My mother was placed at St. Peter's Orphanage. Charlie Sr. told the children that their mother was dead. Of the three children, Stella was the only one who did not buy the story.

The year is 1938, and the depression is in full swing. A massive flood takes its toll on the Mississippi Valley region. Not only are Steinbeck's Oakies moving out of the dust bowl, but also a large group of sharecroppers from Arkansas, Tennessee, and surrounding areas. John Hall and Hessie land in Escalon, California, a small farming community in the Central San Joaquin Valley. Escalon is located a scant eight miles from Modesto where I eventually moved with my adopted family in 1962.

In 1963, Stella found Hessie through an aunt in Saint Louis, Missouri. Stella contacted Grandma ending a search that spanned twenty-five years. Because we both spent a large portion of our lives searching for our mothers, I feel a close kinship with Stella, even though we never met.

Some of the pictures I have from Rosie's collection are of Hessie in Escalon. The street I was raised on in Modesto is two blocks west of McHenry

Boulevard, the road used to travel to Escalon. After Grandma was discovered, the family in Memphis began to visit her. They passed within shouting distance of where I was living.

Grandma's last husband, Ray Whitely, a retired farmer and Baptist minister, is now 99 years old. Grandma lived until she was eighty-four. At the age of seventy-eight, Grandpa Charlie died and was buried in Memphis at the Veteran's Cemetery.

After having made my initial contact with the Scolas, I proceeded to learn about my mother's brother's side of the family.

During my search for the family, many well-meaning individuals recommended the Mormon Genealogy Service. I followed up on this lead only to find out that the Mormon Genealogy Service could not provide me with the information I sought. I was informed that their records were complete up to seventy-five years ago. The bulk of their information comes from the National Census Bureau. Federal law mandates that national census information be classified for seventy-five years. The rest of their information is received from private individuals and several different organizations. The people I dealt with were very courteous and sympathetic. They are a definite asset to our society.

The Scolas gave me Uncle Charlie Kirk's phone number. At the time I received Uncle Charlie's phone number, I was aware that my financial posture had plummeted. I didn't need much, only a little money to cover the costs of transportation to meet the family. I felt I should begin with the Kirk side of the family.

In my reflections on this subject I realized that the events in my life that were truly important have always been accompanied by a materially placed value. I have always taken care of things when money was involved. Wouldn't it be smart to give the family an opportunity to place a value on my return? It certainly would tell me how sincere this side of the family was towards my return.

I asked Uncle Charlie, whom I was to learn was also my godfather, for his help for transportation costs only. He didn't say no, but he didn't say yes either. He did say he would "let me know." He never did help me, and my relationship with him became strained. I will not go into Uncle Charlie's financial situation, but just let me say that I felt he had the resources to help me, and did not. My business was to find out what kind of a family I was a part of. I am isolated from Uncle Charlie's side of the family because of their not showing me that they care. The Scolas care for me and showed it by providing me with the means to come see them. The Kirks provided no such assistance. The reason these two branches of my family have been separated by a wide chasm, that grows year by year, is that one side of the family cares and the other does not.

I arrived in Memphis on a Wednesday morning. The next day, Cousin Ollie drove me the twenty miles south into Mississippi to meet Uncle Charlie. We had given Charlie no warning of our visit. The family agreed that if we did, Charlie wouldn't be there when we arrived.

Ollie and I had a great day together. Ollie has the driest sense of humor I've ever seen and a rich, deep baritone voice that is a pleasure to hear. I enjoyed my first trip into Mississippi immensely.

As we traveled south, I noticed that large quantities of forest were covered with an unusual creeping vine. In several locations the forests and the vines were dead giving them an eerie appearance. Ollie gave me a lesson on the vines and the reason for the dead forests.

Erosion is a major problem in the southern states, especially the states in direct contact with the Mississippi River. Many years ago, several solutions to the erosion were discussed by those concerned with the problem. The Army Corps of Engineers imported Kudzu, a fast growing vine from South America, that they felt would solve the problem of erosion.

Kudzu did exactly what the engineers expected it to do. The only drawback was it spread into the surrounding forests. In the process, it killed off thousands of acres of prime forest. It is now considered a blight on the countryside.

The growth of Kudzu is analogous to the growth of our welfare system. While both started out doing good, they both wound up sucking the host dry. Both the Kudzu and the forest are dead. In the future, the erosion problem will be magnified and tremendous damage will be done. The welfare system is in the process of doing the same to our society. The barrage of taxes, tolls and licenses are sucking our society and the working man dry. Will we experience the same end result in our society as the kudzu and the forests experienced in Mississippi?

The situation is not hopeless. With proper management, we will survive. The proper management is not at this time forthcoming. The county, in which I live, Stanislaus County, has an affectionate nickname known far and wide as Santa Claus County. We no longer have a Marshall's Office. Hundreds of tax producing jobs and essential services have been cut. Our library, necessary for our children's future and as a resource for hundreds of business people, is facing total closure next year. Yet the welfare budget grows along with the amount of taxes we pay. The only ones doing anything about the situation are the larger businesses; they are moving out of the area to communities with more advantageous tax structures.

Uncle Charlie is the only one of Hessie's three

children left. He has run the only towing and sal-
vage yard in De Soto County for many years and is
well known in those parts. I felt that Charlie would
be very helpful in unraveling my family's mysteri-
ous past.

Charlie is a man with thick glasses that distort
his face. His skin color was beet red. He reminded
me of a person who has worked hard all of his life. I
saw no physical resemblance between Charlie and
his two sisters.

"Hello, Uncle Charlie. I'm George," I said
when I first met him.

Charlie was visibly startled by our arrival. His
eyes looked down at the ground for a moment then
looked up again. The whole time he never missed a
coil in the cable he was winding. "Do you have a
birth certificate?" he asked.

This was totally unexpected considering I had
learned he couldn't read. His wife of thirty years had
passed away a few years earlier. She was the one
who did Charlie's paperwork. Without her, his business had declined. I produced the document and
handed it to him. Charlie scrutinized it like he knew
what he was doing. He made no further comments
worth recording on the subject, but the lack of warmth
towards me suggested he felt I was just a kudzu vine
in the family tree.

I met Charlie's daughter, Mary Nell, and his

son, Charlie Jr., while I was there. Neither one of
them made much of an impression on me. I can understand why they are what they are. An apple never
falls far from the tree.

  When Grandma Hessie died, she left her home
in Escalon to Charlie and one Margie Freitas. Upon
my return to Modesto, Charlie wanted me to find
out who Margie was and report back to him. I haven't.

  Charlie Jr. took me over to the county recorder
where I met his ex sister-in-law. Joyce Kirk is one of
the sweetest ladies I have ever met. She was married
to Uncle Charlie's other son. Joyce said that her ex-
husband drank too much. She has a beautiful daughter just starting a career as an airline stewardess.

  I had learned from my juvenile records that
Mom and Dad were married in Hernando, the county
seat. Joyce made a facsimile of Mom and Dad's
marriage certificate giving me proof that I am not a
little bastard. I couldn't treasure that piece of paper
more if it was made of gold.

  One by one I met all the family members living within easy driving range of Memphis. Cousin
Kathy, my mother's namesake was next. She has the
personality most resembling my mother's. She is very
pretty and speaks her mind. Many times, people who
are this forward are viewed as being rude. What is
really being objected to is an airing of the truth. The
accusation of being rude is meant to divert the atten-

tion of anyone listening.

Kathy had an interesting story to tell me. During the period that the State of Tennessee was searching for Mom, November of 1989 through August of 1990, the state sent a letter to Uncle Tony, Kathy's father. The letter was asking for information on the current status of one Kathleen Rheba Curtis. Cousin Kathy is Uncle Tony's right hand. When he showed her the letter, she advised Uncle Tony to contact the state. She wanted to know why after all these years the state should want information on her deceased aunt.

The state answered them in a most unsatisfactory manner. They told the Scolas they could not provide any information. They, however, expected information from Tony and Kathy. Uncle Tony told me he considered hiring an attorney, but later changed his mind. Cousin Kathy kept the fire alive.

Cousin Kathy told me she knew why the state was asking about her aunt. Her intuition told her that her aunt's children were looking for the family. For many years, she had watched my mother sit in her mother's kitchen hour after hour, drinking and crying over the loss of her two children. Once the state contacted Uncle Tony, Kathy knew it would be just a matter of time before her aunt's children would find them.

After Uncle Tony and I finished our initial conversation on the phone, he called Cousin Kathy immediately. It had been two years since the state had contacted the Scolas regarding the whereabouts of Mom. Kathy was at work at the time.

"Guess who just called?" Tony asked.

"Aunt Kathy's kids," was her answer. Here was a young lady, busy at work, her mind occupied with all the responsibilities related to her job at the printing company where she was employed, yet she knew who had called Uncle Tony.

What a sweet old boy Uncle Tony is! It was his home and Stella's that opened up to my mother when she needed a place to stay for the first twenty-three days of my life.

During my stay in Memphis, Cousin Rosie and Ollie took me there. The home is gone. All that is left is a vacant lot. But at one point it had been a corner grocery store with apartments upstairs. Behind the grocery store was a stable. The stable was used to house the beasts of burden that pulled the produce wagons that were a part of the family business. I wonder if Mom ever took me to see the animals in the stable.

The most important conversation during my three-week stay in Memphis was with Uncle Tony. He confirmed my suspicions that were raised by the juvenile records, that during my infancy with Mom in no condition to take care of Sis and me, and Dad

in Korea, he and Stella applied to the Tennessee
Children's Home Society to adopt us. He said that
Georgia Tann turned them down. This sadness was
carried in his heart for forty years until the light of
goodness shined on him.

He felt that he and Stella could have provided
a good home for Sis and me. He told me several times
that he could have done better for us. Unfortunately
he did not know the kinds of people he was dealing
with in the persons of Georgia Tann and Camille
Kelly.

Family ties were much stronger in that era than
they are now. Families were closer and took better
care of each other. There wasn't a social state like
we have in the nineties. Uncle Sam was alive and
well. Now we are dealing with Daddy Sam. The family unit bonds are weak or nonexistent. All this has
come about in the time it has taken me to reach the
age of forty-four.

Tony and Stella were turned down for "economic reasons." Uncle Tony has assured me that they
had both the material means and emotional resources
to nurture two more children. While telling me this,
Uncle Tony's voice cracked and he began to cry. I
love you Uncle Tony.

Uncle Tony died a short time ago. How ironic
that the first one to welcome me back after four decades is the first one to go. He was a caring man that

I am proud to call "Uncle".

CHAPTER SEVENTEEN
A Place Called Home

Sunday quickly arrived. The first week went incredibly fast. By now I had met most of the family members and visited the graves of others. In my possession was a small booty of pictures, important documents, answers to questions I had dreamed of for years and most important of all, a family. A reunion was planned for Sunday that would give me the opportunity to meet those family members I had not yet met.

One by one the family arrived: uncles, cousins, second cousins and third cousins. Unfortunately there were no aunts. The house soon overflowed into the front and back yards. Children were playing, people who hadn't seen each other for years embraced, and many tears of happiness were shed. Food was in ample supply, cameras were flashing and camcorders were rolling as various groups of the family went about the house visiting. I could see my efforts paying off.

Several family members had believed for years that my father had taken Sis and me with him. This curious rumor was dispelled, and in return I learned several facts about my father. He had been a pool player and a lady's man with superior athletic abilities. As was intimated in the juvenile record, he didn't pay child support, rent or other bills he could get away with. The picture presented was of an irresponsible person. The picture also looked a lot like me. I attribute much of this to genetics.

One regret I have about this reunion is that my sister did not attend. Throughout my visit, the most asked question was "What about your sister, Margaret (Kathy) Each time this question echoed through my mind, I shuddered. I had wanted so much for Sis to be a part of discovering our real family. When she and I were suffering through our Hell on earth and knowing we were adopted, we made a pledge to each other to find our real family. Now the family was found, and I was unable to convince Sis that it still mattered.

Somewhere down the rocky road of life, Sis lost her focus on our pledge. I believe Kathy's way of dealing with the harsh realities of life was to bury her pain deep within her subconscious. She took the road of denial. It is easier to bury pain than to confront it and defeat it. Like the planting of Kudzu to stop erosion, the short-term objectives were met, but the long-range damage would couple with time to destroy a dream.

Alcohol was my kudzu, and so it was with Sis as well. She has been without a drink for two years. But her dream of finding the family is still lost and may never be found. She has never had the perspective of being a parent. It is possible that this missing piece in her life contributes to her indifference to my finding the family. She has said many times that if our biological family had loved us, they would have kept us. This is just not so. There is no correlation between love and intelligence. Mom exercised her intelligence, putting our welfare ahead of wanting to keep us. The reason for our having been adopted has been explained to Kathy, but she continues to ignore the facts. Kathy doesn't understand the concept of a parent being separated from their children. She doesn't know that of all the pains one can suffer in life, this is the most damaging. Being a divorced, non-custodial parent, I am truly aware of this pain and its consequences.

When asked over and over about the absence of Kathy at the reunion, these thoughts ran through my mind, but I was unable to communicate them to my newfound relatives. Instead, I would say, "I don't know about Sis, perhaps someday." I do hope that in the near future she will be able to meet the fine people who comprise our family in the Memphis area.

In the meantime, I basked in the love of a family gathered together to discover what it had missed for forty years. This reunion with my family was bought with my sweat and tears. I couldn't let anything spoil it.

Rosie and I had invited Denny to our family

reunion. Denny, in her own devilishly sweet way, said she would love to come, however she had a previous engagement. She would be able to rendezvous with us the following week. Arrangements were made to meet at Applebees, a very nice restaurant in Memphis.

I was stunned when I first met Denny Glad. I had expected to find a woman with a physique to match her powerful personality. Instead, I found out that it is indeed true that small packages hold large presents. She was so stimulating; she gave me a natural high just being in her presence. Somewhere in our conversation I proposed to her. I don't understand why she said no. I put on my best "crushed heart" expression, and we laughed ourselves silly. We did hug and exchange cordial, socially polite kisses.

I felt an immediate bonding with Denny. She represents a woman of the rarest beauty, a beauty of the heart. An additional attraction for me is that we both share the common goal of modifying the adoption secrecy laws. I am sure that Denny's late husband would be proud to see her continuing, what I believe to be, an ongoing miracle. As of November 6, 1993, by her own conservative estimation, nearly fifteen hundred victims have been reunited with their families.

Nearly two years have passed since I first observed Denny Glad being interviewed by Mike Wallace on Sixty Minutes. Our relationship has grown during this time. It would be a great honor to see Denny and her associates receive the credit due them for the work they have accomplished.

Tann and Kelley wrought a massive evil with their scam. The evil they and others throughout history have done has not altered mankind's intelligence or its goodness. It takes time, but the enemies of goodness are doomed to defeat. However, we cannot cause evil to be extinct. We can only contain it. Man needs to contain and control evil better than we have. If not, we will meet our doom. Prevention is our only salvation.

On June 1, 1990, I received initial biological information about myself, from the State of Tennessee. This information was gleaned from the sealed adoption records, in Nashville, which originated at the Tennessee Children's Home Society in Memphis. These records stated that my mother was Scottish and Dad was German. They neglected to state that Native-American, Spanish, and Greek blood also ran through my veins!

I can remember watching movies that depicted the U.S. Cavalry chasing red-blooded savages that supposedly had raped and scalped white settlers. In later years, this erroneous idea would be replaced with the truth, but, during my childhood, Native-

Americans were given a negative representation in our society. During this same time, the Spanish were viewed as being a lazy, unkempt, and ignorant people.

Not everyone felt this way, but, when putting babies up for sale, the sellers would want the records to reflect nationalities that they felt were more saleable. Adopting couples, when given a choice, would most likely take a Scottish/German baby rather than one with Native-American, Spanish, or Greek nationality.

Tann and Waldour realized this and that's why my records were changed to read Scottish/German, leaving out the Indian/Spanish/Greek parentage. I now know that I was at the Tennessee Children's Home Society for one reason only, and that reason was—SALE!

CHAPTER EIGHTEEN
Saint Peter's Home For Children

In the past, Poplar Avenue in Memphis could have easily been nicknamed, "Orphan Row." I know of at least three orphanages which were located on Poplar - The Convent of the Good Shepherd, Saint Peter's, and TCHS. Of the three, only St. Peter's still stands, though it is in an altered state these days concentrating more on the elderly than young orphans.

My visit at this time revealed that the people currently working there are just as indifferent as those who worked there during my visit in 1982. Ninety percent of the time when I have told people of my life dream coming true, they are happy I have found my family. Their behavior reflects it. It was not so with these people. I felt I was being treated more as a bad memory come back to haunt them. Their lips were sealed tightly against discussion of the TCHS scandal. Why? If they have nothing to fear, they should have welcomed my triumphant return. The only exceptions to this behavior were Mary Wilson and Father Joe Palozzi.

I have just received a reply to a letter sent to Senator Douglas Henry's office regarding the portion of the Tennessee adoption laws dealing with residency requirements. In the wake of the TCHS scandal, the legislature supposedly reinstated the residency requirement in 1951. Apparently, the law stated that any child of Tennessee could not be adopted unless the adoptive parents were residents of Tennessee. According to Ms. Austin, the Nashville Tennesseean, dated February 14, 1951, stated that this statute took effect that year.

In order to confirm that the law did take effect in 1951, I sent a request to the Office of Legal Services for the State of Tennessee. The reply took three weeks from the time I sent my letter. According to the letter, an amendment had been added to the Adoption Act of 1951, but not until 1959. What does the Adoption Act of 1951, say, and why, with such a scandal and so many children being hurt, had they not immediately added the residency requirement by amendment in 1951? I sent another letter asking for clarification, but have not received any reply.

Here is the letter I received concerning my initial request:

Dear Mr. Curtis:
I am writing at the request of Senator Douglas Henry.
Under present law, Tennessee Code Annotated, Section 35-1-105(c), requires that a person seeking to adopt a Tennessee child must have lived or maintained a regular place of abode in

*Tennessee for one year prior to filing
of the adoption petition. This residency
requirement was inserted into the Adoption Act of 1951 (Chapter 202 of the
Public Acts of 1951) by amendment in
1959 (Chapter 223, sec. 1, Public Acts
of 1959). Under the 1959 amendment,
although petitioners in adoption proceedings are not required to make Tennessee their legal residence, they are
required to "have lived, maintained a
home and been physically present in
Tennessee, or on federal territory within
the present boundaries of Tennessee for
one (1) year next preceding the filing
of the petition...."*

Sis and I were adopted April/May of 1952. Our
adoptive parents were residents of Michigan. How
could this adoption have taken place if the residency
requirement was actually in the Adoption Act of
1951? This was very likely an illegal adoption on
the heels of the new adoption law. Did St. Peter's, a
religious institution run by the Catholic Church,
knowingly break the law? And what about a family
denied permission to adopt its own children, children eventually shipped out of state when their own
family could have cared for them. We know how this

could have happened, and very likely did happen, in light of the scandal and the way Crumps people had previously voided the residency requirement law. That law should definitely have been reaffirmed immediately at the time of the scandal. Were the same politicians again playing ostrich with children's lives?

I have asked for help to figure out how this could have happened. None has been forthcoming from St. Peter's. This leads me to believe that there are people who have done something they do not want to be held accountable for. Monsignor Kearney, a Roman Catholic prelate, a member of the board of directors at TCHS, the prelate whose name appears on my baptismal certificate, may have taken more to his grave than anyone will ever know.

If I had been Georgia Tann, every time I drove down Poplar Avenue, I would have salivated at the thought of all the money on the hoof at St. Peter's and at the Convent of the Good Shepherd. It is quite possible Tann's mind conceived methods to use the children of these two homes, to her advantage, as she used those at TCHS.

St. Peter's must have known what was going on. In view of the recent revelations of scandals involving Catholic priests, bishops and even cardinals, it is quite possible that someone in the church, possibly Kearney, had a hand in what was going on at TCHS. It is also quite possible that there was some involvement by St. Peter's. I emphasize that this is all conjecture, but after what so many others and I have been through, it is not out of the question.

Doris told me that as a toddler, I had sat on a gas heater. That is where the large scar on my leg supposedly came from. There are no medical records to verify this. How could she have known for sure if it was not in my medical records?

I have already recounted how I felt a consuming fear whenever John or Doris mentioned sending me back to the orphanage. In my trip back in 1982, I felt only good feelings upon my visit to St. Peter's. On this trip, I felt the same. I felt the familiarity one feels with visiting a place one lived as a child. There was no terror in my mind.

A visit to St. Joseph's Hospital, the place of my birth, was not on the agenda in 1982. It was included on this trip. While walking up the steps, I began to feel a tightening in my chest. My mind reeled and traveled back to a time of terror. I remembered an intense pain and a figure standing at the top of the steps. I remembered a fear of entering this building. This experience leads me to believe that St. Joseph's was the place I was afraid to go back to, not St. Peter's. St. Joseph's was probably the hospital that treated me for the large burn that scarred my leg.

I will never know exactly what happened to

me, or even where it actually happened, just as we will never know all the players and their roles in the TCHS scandal. Too many participants have died and too many records have been destroyed for us to ever be certain. But we must continue to uncover whatever is left to uncover so we may know what steps to take to insure this never happens again.

CHAPTER NINETEEN
Sweet Sorrow and A Happy Return

The thought of staying on in Memphis never crossed my mind. There were too many loose ends to be taken care of including finding Dad. I had hit a blank wall in Memphis regarding this. Not one of my relatives in Memphis had heard anything about Dad's whereabouts. I knew finding him would take a lot of work.

Another reason I couldn't leave was Andrew. My children, especially young Andrew, are my number one priority. Andrew needs to have me around, as all children need the influence of both their male and female parents. I don't see him as often as I should despite a court ordered visitation agreement. Andy and I want to spend more time together. Only one obstacle prevents this. I won't mention names. Infrequent as our visits are, he still needs me. Finding Dad and being there for my son were the most important of all the reasons for my return to Modesto.

My stay in Memphis accomplished many things. The most important took place inside of me with my attitude. I had constantly lived in the past, going over and over all the bad events in my life and wondering why me? With this trip, I began to see the future and live in the present. Instead of carrying the weight of the world on my back and wasting precious mental energy on the past over which I have no control, I was now planning for the future. An important part of my past had been found, and I was beginning to experience the incredibly delicious emotions of contentment.

Cousin Joe Scola and his wife, Joan, drove me to the Amtrak station. Hugs and kisses were sorrowfully exchanged. I was prepared for the sadness. It was not the end of the world, a perception I used to experience when I had achieved other goals in life. This was but a beginning for me.

At 10:30 in the evening, "The City of New Orleans", chugged north with me aboard. Sleep softly came to me. I did not have to deal with all the anxieties of the trip out.

I awoke just before sunrise as we crossed Illinois. Looking east across the flatlands of the "Land of Lincoln," I saw the sun casually breach the horizon. Slowly it rose in triumphant grandeur heralding another day in the life of mankind.

I did some sightseeing on the return trip, but most of the time was used to sort out what had happened in Memphis and to plan for my assault on the wall between Dad and me. I made a list of possible avenues of locating him and what I would need to do to traverse each one. By my arrival home, the list was fairly long.

As expected, Karen was at the station when I

arrived in Riverbank. We gave each other a long embrace, probably each wondering what was going on in the other's mind. We went to her place first, partly to pick up the portable valuables I had stored there against a break-in at my house while I was absent. The other purpose was to allow Karen to be the first to view the reunion tape and hear the story of my adventure. This we accomplished from atop her bed with the Davis girls accompanying us. And yes, I did behave myself.

For a period of several weeks after my return, I sat back and enjoyed a well-earned rest. The post reunion euphoria was quite enjoyable. I contacted an old friend of mine, Charlie Mills. I cannot remember the reason, but it was fortuitous.

Charlie had dated my sister twenty some years earlier. When I left for my induction into the Air Force, he sang at my going away party. He was a very nice man then and continues to be.

Charlie needed help with his recycling business, and I needed a job. This business arrangement has gone on to both our benefits for two years. Until he reads this book, Charlie will not realize the part he has played in making this book possible. The job he gave me earns me enough money to support myself. Just as important, it allows me the time I need to work on the manuscript. It only takes me two hours a day to complete my job. The rest of the time is freed up to work on the book. I look forward to the time when I can present him with a copy of "Tennessee Tears."

CHAPTER TWENTY
Desperately Seeking Dad

I spent a lot of time goofing off at first. An idea would pop into my mind about how to locate Dad, I would make a phone call, find a dead end and go back to goofing off. I did start writing this book during this time, but I was not yet seriously into it. This lackadaisical attitude lasted until December when an acquaintance of mine told me of an article appearing in the Modesto Bee. This article led to my coming into contact with Rhonda, a college student whom I hope to meet some day. With her help, God bless her, I learned a great deal about the years my family spent in Bluefield, West Virginia. Following is the information I received, thanks to her help.

Until 1950, the telephone directory listed several Curtises. Along with the phone numbers, the occupations of the Curtises were also noted. Through the old Bluefield phone directory I learned my father was an employee of the "Smokehouse," a local beer and wine pub with several pool tables. George J. Curtis, my grandfather, operated the "Doughboy Restaurant." My Great Uncle Gus ran "The Top Hat Cafe" at 130 Princeton Ave., Bluefield, West Virginia.

My paternal side had a lot in common with my maternal family. They all operated businesses downstairs and lived in the flats above. How smart!

Grandpa and a friend of his, Paul Chryssikos, were secretaries of a local Greek organization called American Hellenic Education Progressive Association (AHEPA). Paul is alive and well, and I will talk kindly of him and his friend Frank Roupas shortly. By all accounts, it was going well for my family. The addition of a grandchild, Margaret Katherine Curtis, my sister, I'm sure brought great joy into their lives. The family received a couple of visitors from Memphis, my cousins Rosalie and Joe Scola Jr., who were about nine and ten at the time. When I met them in Memphis, they told me they remembered how they peeked through the keyholes to watch the adults' party.

Rhonda checked the 1951 directory. The Curtis family had disappeared from the pages. It only meant that they had moved, but why?

The answer to this question lies in the mechanization that hit Bluefield at this time. In 1950, Bluefield had roughly 24,000 inhabitants. Mechanization of the coal mining industry forced laborers to seek work elsewhere. When the workers moved, they took their stomachs. My family followed in order to stay in business feeding those stomachs. Bluefield, located in the heart of the Pocahontas Coal Mines is now a shadow of its bustling past.

I felt that by getting in touch with Paul Chryssikos, I might be able to learn where the family had moved. Paul is a very handsome man with great intelligence. His focus and clarity of speech does not betray the fact that he has attained an excess of eighty years. Rhonda gave me his phone number, and I bought more stock in the phone company. Paul, I learned, had taught a Greek culture class at the college level. Unfortunately, he had lost touch with my family, but he was able to enlighten me about my family history.

The Curtis clan was originally from a little city one hundred twenty five miles north of Athens, Karpinisi. Karpanisi is in the state of Evratania. The family's true name is Kourtis. My Greek name is Georgios Jani Kourtis. When my grandfather came through Ellis Island, the family name was heard as Curtis by the "anglo" ears. If this sounds familiar, it is because it is the exact same problem that was encountered by the Bubnes (Urbanes) family.

Paul and I have written each other and exchanged photographs. He related many more facts to me about my family, but nothing was as important as his referral to his friend, Frank Roupas.

Grandpa George was part of one of the largest immigrations in history. As with many migrations, religious freedom was the cause. The Ottoman Empire, an anti-Christian state, forced many a Greek to flee. Thousands of Greeks came to the United States. Initially they settled along the Eastern Seaboard.

Eventually, they journeyed southward seeking employment and more favorable weather.

Grandpa started his family in Washington D. C., the place of my father's birth. The family left Washington for the bounty of the coal fields in West Virginia.

In order to locate Dad, I tried various Greek organizations. I tried the Cathedral of Saint Sophia in Washington where most Greeks were baptized. Luck was not with me. I next tried the Greek Orthodox North American Diocese in New York, the Greek consulates in Los Angeles and Washington, and American Hellenic Education Progressive Association. I even tried the local Greek Church where I made the acquaintance of several parishioners. Still no luck!

I wrote to the mayor of Karpinisi. I am still waiting for a reply over a year later. I contacted the Bluefield paper, and they tried to help by running a story about my search for the family. Several people responded with tidbits of information, but none of it was helpful.

Dad's service number was in my juvenile record. I contacted my local congressman's office. The Honorable Gary Condit demonstrated a sincere desire to help, but they had to deal with other government agencies. They tried the Military Records Center in St. Louis. Unfortunately, a fire had destroyed many of the records. My dad's records were among those destroyed. I even tried a 1-900 number that dealt with ex-servicemen. Dad had been in Korea. This organization researched his Korean unit but was unable to locate it.

A friend advised me in December of 1992, that Lifetime Cable was going to air a movie on March 25, 1993. The movie was called "Stolen Babies." It was about TCHS and starred Mary Tyler Moore who subsequently won an Emmy for her stirring performance as Georgia Tann. I am so naive at times. I actually believed that I could have this book written, published and released in conjuncture with the airing of the movie. I dove into the manuscript. This single act eventually proved to be both my salvation and the key to finding Dad.

On January 14, 1993, cousin Kathy flew out from Memphis and disembarked from the plane with a book of matches in one hand and a cigarette in the other. We hugged and kissed before walking to a cafe in the terminal that allowed smoking. We talked for awhile before strolling to my car in the parking lot.

There were so many places I wanted to take cousin Kathy. How to do it in four days would take some creative scheduling. She had never flown in a jet before and had never gone beyond the immediate geographical area where she was raised. She knew nothing about California except that it is the hippie/

music center of the cosmos.

Since we were so close to the ocean, I decided to make Half Moon Bay our first stop. I headed west on Highway 92. As we crossed the coastal range, Kathy kept exclaiming about how big the mountains out here are. I couldn't help laughing, not at her, but with her. Her innocent child-like behavior was sweet. I informed her that these were just foothills compared to the Sierras we would be visiting in a few days.

We made it to the coast. The Pacific lay before us on a clear, blustery day. Visibility was unlimited. We could see ocean freighters sailing toward port in San Francisco Harbor. I remembered the excitement of my introduction to the grandeur of the Pacific Ocean. Kathy's reactions reminded me of that feeling.

Off came the shoes and socks. The waves rolled in, and Kathy's toes were covered with salty brine. It didn't take long for reality to set in, and she quickly retreated to dry off her cold feet.

I would take cousin Kathy all over the place on her visit. We would visit the snowcapped Sierras, Grandma Hessie's widower, Ray Whitely, and Grandma Hessie's grave. But cousin Kathy's introduction to my sister Kathy would be the highlight of her trip.

As we were driving back over the Altamont

from visiting the Pacific, I saw the plan unfold in its
entire cunning and charming splendor. I explained it
carefully to cousin Kathy. We were both laughing
like giddy little kids. The final touch of the plan was
agreed upon just as we reached Modesto.

We slid into the parking lot at "Jack's on D"
street where Sis was working. Over the years I.have
been irritated by my sister pretending to listen to me
when she wasn't. It was now payback time! Sis knew
that cousin Kathy was due to arrive soon. If she had
paid attention she would have known the day, and if
she had cared, she would have asked just to be sure.
She did neither

According to the plan, cousin Kathy entered
the lounge and took a seat at the end of the bar. After
a five-minute wait, I walked in to the usual chorus of
good-natured ribbing I would always get. Cousin
Kathy is a very attractive and petite woman, and she
easily caught the eyes of the male patrons. I said hello
to all my buddies and sat down at the opposite end
of the bar from cousin Kathy. Sis was busy serving
Cousin a drink, and as I knew she would, Cousin
had attracted everyone's attention.

In a low voice I explained to those at my end
of the bar that the pretty lady down at the other end
was our cousin just in from Memphis. I told them
Sis was unaware of who the lady was, and we were
going to have a little fun.

George John Curtis   238

I called to Sis to get her attention. When she
looked my way, I motioned for her to come over.
When she did I bent over the counter and, in a clan-
destine voice, asked her who that cute woman was.
She answered, "You've got to stop chasing women!"
"It's a dirty job, but someone has to do it," I replied.
The whole time cousin Kathy was giving a performance deserving of an Emmy. After several minutes went by, and the time was right, I did my best
Bogart move and strolled casually across the room
to cousin Kathy. I engaged her in a casual conversation for a few moments then started rubbing her back;
a common ploy of the male gender when meeting a
female at a bar. "Do you think Sis suspects anything?" I quietly asked. "No, but she did tell me that
the guy at the end of the bar is harmless." I was
shocked! I knew she meant me. "Sis, did you tell
this poor unsuspecting woman that I am harmless?"
Sis positioned herself right in front of us and said,
"What can I say?" "You can start by saying hello to
cousin Kathy from Memphis," I replied.

I wish there had been a camera in my hand to
record the expression on my sister's face. Sis walked
around the end of the bar, and they embraced and
began to cry. I was busy laughing my head off. As
all this was going on, the patrons who had been let
in on the joke clapped their hands and shouted, "hooray!" "Hooray!"

Cousin Kathy visited the next two days at Sis' house. It was my hope that Sis would develop a stronger yearning to meet the rest of the family, but that hasn't happened yet.

I bid farewell to cousin Kathy at S. F. International. From the entrance of the terminal, I watched her little silhouette disappear into the throng of people boarding the plane. I cried because I love her, and I will miss her until I see her again.

Located between the two cerebral hemispheres is the Limbic System. The Limbic System controls the amount of dopamine released into the neurological pathways that carry billions of bytes of information to areas such as vision, hearing, etc. When an excess amount of stress enters the brain, the Limbic System will cease its supply of dopamine to the neurotransmitters preventing the brain from overloading itself. It blocks recall and the search process ceases.

An example of this is if you see a face of a familiar actor, for instance, your brain begins a search for that information. Someone asks you, "Who is that actor?" The stress brought on by this question begins a shutdown of the search process. You think harder in order to compensate, and the process shuts down even more. The process continues in a downward spiral until it becomes impossible to remember the actor's name. Yet sometime later, after the stress has been removed and while you are doing something totally unrelated, the name you were searching for pops into your head.

By the time cousin Kathy had arrived, I was totally stressed out by my search for Dad. I was unable to think anymore. Then came Cousin's visit. Following her visit, I turned immediately to my book. No sooner did this happen than the key to finding Dad occurred to me. Up until this time, the main stumbling block was the absence of his exact birth date. It stated in my juvenile records that Dad and Mom were involved in a brawl at "The Brass Rail". I was also there, tucked away in Mom's womb. It hit me, no pun intended that since Dad was arrested, there should be a record of that arrest. I knew that one of the primary pieces of information an arrest record contains is the birth date of the person arrested. My earlier urge to write off "The Brass Rail" as unimportant was wrong. The key was there all the time.

I toyed with the idea all weekend, knowing that it would be difficult to do anything until Monday morning. As I dialed the number of the Memphis Police Department, my hands shook. It took them some time to locate the records, but even though it had been forty-four years, they still had my dad on file.

I couldn't wait to send off my letter to the Vital Statistics Office in Washington, D.C. with my check enclosed to cover the cost of the record search. Unfortunately, in my haste to mail the letter, I forgot to put down the month of my father's birth. The letter came back to me a few days later with the check still enclosed.

I initially cursed the Office of Vital Statistics, but after I calmed down, I saw that it was my own fault. Hastily I made the needed correction and mailed the letter again. This time every thing went as expected. After a few days of waiting, I received Dad's birth certificate.

I came to the realization that there was no way I could finish the book in time to be released in conjunction with "Stolen Babies." I knew I had to somehow keep writing so I wouldn't lose my momentum. On the other hand, I was now in possession of the key to finding Dad.

I checked with Cheri Matthews, the lovely reporter at The Modesto Bee who did the initial story on me. Through her, The Modesto Bee was convinced to do another story on me and announce the upcoming airing of "Stolen Babies." The local cable company also agreed to have me as a guest on a half-hour program with an interview format. The program is aired twice weekly. The Bee article mentioned the cable program in addition to the movie. The idea was to keep the issue in the news and to make myself known so it would be easier to get my book published. In short, I wanted to establish credibility.

My writing skills have never been equal to a Steinbeck or a Hemingway. I struggled with the manuscript until a friend of mine, Ira White, came to my rescue. He agreed to take what I had written, edit it into the proper format, and help me finish the book.

Ira had been collaborating with me on the book for several months when the subject of birthdays came up. It was then that he innocently stated that his birthday was September 15, 1950, the exact day Georgia Tann died! Out of curiosity I wanted a copy of Tann's death certificate to find her exact time of death so I could compare it to Ira's time of birth. I am also curious about the exact cause of death. When I contacted the State of Tennessee I was told that death certificates in the State of Tennessee were classified documents for fifty years, which works out to the year 2000.

With Ira busy writing from the materials I had researched, my manuscript, notes, and interviews he did with me, I had some time freed up to finish my task of finding Dad. From the beginning, I had an ace in the hole, which I chose not to use. Instead, I took my Grandmother's name, Margaret Magner, and began to call all the Magners I could find. I searched Memphis, Camden, Greece, Washington, D.C., West Virginia, any place I could think of that my grandmother's side of the family could be living. The only results were that my·phone bill reached four figures.

I did get in touch with a man named James Magner who proved to be a total gentleman and quite knowledgeable as well. With his help, I was able to learn much about this side of my family.

One of the Magners made Richard Cornwalis pretty angry. He was so angry, he squashed the family and took away their castle and land. Feeling a bit unwanted, the Magners moved to the new world where Cornwalis couldn't touch them.

Like so many new arrivals, they settled in New England and gradually moved south. A few moved west to Indiana and Ohio. Around 1920, the Magners and the Curtises were united by the marriage of my grandmother and grandfather. Grandpa was sixteen years older than Grandma. According to the birth certificate, Dad was the first child produced by this union. There were three more children to come later: Stella, Buddy and Anna Lee.

I had already seen from my juvenile records that my father was not totally responsible. I now learned from an additional source of his irresponsibility. This did not surprise me at this point. However, knowing that I, too, have been guilty of irresponsibility, I wondered if somewhere along the rocky road of life, there had been changes for Dad as there had for me.

There was hope based on genetics. I had discovered that most of the males on my father's side grew up to pursue careers in teaching, military service and clerical service. As already documented, I served in the military and was a teacher. In addition, I wanted to be a priest when I was little. There was hope that the same biological clock that woke me up to tell me to start being responsible had also affected my father. I prayed this would be so.

Every attempt I made to find my father met with failure. Only my own hardheadedness kept me from using my ace in the hole. In a way, I was afraid to use it because there was always the possibility that this ace would fail me as well. In order to calm myself down, I came up with plan "B" just in case. Plan "B" would call for the completion of my book and a trip around the talk show circuit. I was certain that if all else failed, someone who knew Dad would see the show, if Dad didn't see it himself, and either tell him about it or get in contact with me. The premise the plan was based on was that Dad would want to see me after all these years.

On April 1, 1993, I sent my ace the money needed to locate my father. I cannot divulge the name of my operative. This person has helped many others. If they remain anonymous, they will be able to continue helping other people. I would love to give this person the credit they deserve, but I am sure they understand and agree with my decision.

For four weeks, I waited. April 28 arrived just like any other day in my life. The phone rang, startling me. I didn't know who it could be so early in the morning. Then the thought crossed my mind that it was the call I had been waiting for. Bingo!

Ace's sweet voice greeted me. Dad was alive! Had Dad been deceased, Social Security, by law, would have been able to tell me. As it turns out, he lives in Norfolk, Virginia. In addition, I was given both his home and business phone numbers. The business number was to a restaurant and lounge Dad owned in Norfolk called, "The Stonehouse".

I thanked Ace and put the phone down. Almost instantaneously I was hit by a double whammy of jubilation and fear. I would have to fly for the first time in years. In the past, I would get drunk to alleviate my fears. This trip I would not be able to drink or smoke. I could see myself, eyes bulging and nails chewed to the quick, trying to cope with the flight across the country.

But what about Dad? He was sixty-eight. Would his heart be able to take it? Would he want to see me? Would he want to be my father? How could I approach him without scaring him away? I decided to wait until the next day to give me time to think of how to approach Dad.

Paranoia was deteriorating into dementia when

I made up my mind the next day to just call and get it over with. I dialed his number, but it was busy. I redialed. Damn! It was still busy. I was getting ready to bail out. I couldn't stand it anymore. I tried again. After two rings, someone answered, " Stonehouse Restaurant-Lounge, may I help you?" He sounded about the same age as myself. "Yes," I said, "Is John G. Curtis in?" "Speaking," he answered. Suddenly, I couldn't speak. My lips moved, but no sound came out. My brain was whirling with all the clever things I had thought I would say to my dad when I first contacted him, but nothing could be pried out. "Are you sitting down?" I finally asked. "Yes," he replied. I almost felt that he knew it was his son. "My name is George John Curtis, and I believe you are my father."

The silence that greeted me from this person three thousand miles away spoke of the shock he was experiencing. "Oh," was all he managed to say.

I began to tell Dad the story leading up to this moment in as organized a fashion as I could muster. Patiently, he listened. Then, a few phrases into the story, he began filling in the blanks for me. I had done my homework. I wanted Dad to know this. It would have been devastating had he thought I was a fraud, so I made it impossible for him to think this could be so. We would both need a couple of days to sort out our thoughts after this conversation. I told

Dad I would mail him copies of all the documentation I had gathered, and we ended our first conversation.

What I had sought so desperately, I had found.

CHAPTER TWENTY ONE
The Let Down

Before I met with Mom's side of the family, I had promised myself I would follow a course of action I had designed to keep myself from spiraling down into a deep depression. Up until this point, my objectives had been met, even exceeded. The ease with which I had slid into Mother's side of the family, the love and caring I had found there and the acceptance from most of that side of the family, none of which I had been expecting, lulled me into forgetting my objectives. In fact, I had new objectives, set impossibly high and subconsciously designed to optimize the possibility of failure. In short, I expected the same attention, the same immediate acceptance, from Dad's side of the family that I had received in Memphis. Aren't all human beings alike?

Deep inside me was a boiling pot of anger. A few months earlier I had written a few pages in my notebook that I gave to Ira for background information for the story. There was a violence in these pages that I had to express on paper in order to keep from actually acting it out. The scene I wrote about was the murder of my father. When Ira read it, he gave me a call and asked about it. He had thought it was written about my adopted father, John Bubnes. To his surprise, I set him straight. It took some time and a little explaining before he understood the anger towards my real father that had built up inside me. Eventually, he came to realize that it was just like the anger seen in children whose parents have died, the child blames them for something beyond their control. The absence of a parent is like a rejection of the child, no matter how it happens.

From Dad, I learned I have a half sister, Alice, from his second marriage. She was twenty-nine at the time, single and expecting a child in September. She works for Dad, second in charge of "The Stonehouse." Her mother had died at age thirty some-thing. She had also lost a child, a little baby boy who died shortly after his birth. When Dad was telling me about Alice, I could tell by the tone of his voice that he was proud of her.

Much of what Dad had told me on the phone was about our bloodlines and confirmed what I had already learned from other sources. He didn't have any phone numbers or addresses of his siblings or any other members of the family. It was evident his side of the family wasn't very close.

I told him Mom was dead. He said he was sorry to hear that. He had learned of her death years ago when he met up with a mutual friend. The relatives in Memphis all wished me the best in finding Dad, but Dad never asked about them.

Dad told me that when he returned from Korea, he had gone to St. Peter's to find Sis and me. His story paralleled the same problems I had encountered in locating the family; sealed records, and sealed lips.

Dad's current wife, Bonnie, is his third. They have been married for a long time. My stepmother is three months younger than I. She has a daughter by another union. Dad adopted her when he and Bonnie were first married. Though they remain married, they have been separated four years.

Dad had denied me nothing. He had given me all the information he had on the family and had given me a date, September 1, for my arrival to meet the family. I was not treated as an impostor. I was free to enjoy the attainment of a lifelong dream.

I sent the documents to my father as I had said I would. It was important to me that there be no doubt in his mind about me. I know it was a shock to him to hear from a son forty-four years lost, and I know also that there must have been a little skepticism in his mind. I also know there are people debased enough to pull a scam like this on someone.

My next step was to tell Sis. Sis showed no emotion at all. She wasn't curious in the least about the family. I was disappointed in her, but after her response to finding Mom's side of the family, I wasn't surprised.

In the next few days after my first phone call to Dad, I talked to Alice, my half-sister, and to Bonnie, my step-mom, who is twenty-four years younger than Dad. Bonnie sounded so sweet on the phone - a genuine caring woman. She lives in the house that Dad had bought several years earlier. I wondered why they had separated.

Dad had a drinking problem, Bonnie told me. The odor his body gave off at night while he was sleeping was the reason given for their separation. Dad had a studio apartment built onto the back of his business for him to live in. I wondered why Dad didn't just sleep in a separate bedroom. I thought there had to be more to this than was being told to me.

I expected a courtesy call from Norfolk after the documents had arrived. That is how I think. It is the correct way of doing things, if you care. There was no phone call, no letter. Nothing! I felt rejected.

My intuition told me my father hadn't received the package. Dad had instructed me to send it to his

house where Bonnie lives. The spiral of rejection
slowed enough for me to realize Bonnie probably
went through the package first and hadn't given it to
Dad yet. A call to Bonnie verified this suspicion.

I don't like sitting around waiting for things
to happen. I called Dad a couple of days later and
found out that he had received the documents and
examined them. I felt he would open up to me more
now that I had provided the proof of my claim. Instead, I became painfully aware that Dad was going
to remain detached. The gap between Dad and myself was growing wider. If I had only him to deal
with, it would be possible to work things out eventually. But he had traitors in his own camp.

I was curious about my half-sister, Alice, so I
connected with her. I found a confused young lady.
She is a sweet young woman with great potential.
She is also physically beautiful like my sister Kathy.
Alice informed me not to be alarmed by Dad's lack
of attentiveness. He treats her that way, also. She told
me that while she was hospitalized for a few days,
he visited her only once. She also told me he doesn't
call her very often. As far as the business goes, Alice
told me it wasn't much. She works there and knows
everything about the operation. Whenever he can
force himself from "The Stonehouse," he likes to play

golf. I also learned he is smart when it comes to his business. In the bar business, if you aren't careful and watch the operation closely, the bartenders can rob you blind.

My philosophy in life, regarding personal contacts, is to call once. Next time is their turn to call. If my call isn't returned, I give them the benefit of the doubt and contact them again. If they do not return the second call, I don't call them again. I could not bring myself to do this with Dad. I had already called him four times!

A short period of time, perhaps a month, quickly raced by. I received no letters, no pictures and no encouragement from my father. "He doesn't give a damn," was my recurring thought during this time. I kept comparing his behavior now to his behavior in the past. I know he was in the military and overseas at the time Mom, Kathy and I were having problems. Having been in the military, I know this to be no excuse. The military gives special exemptions to those members of the armed forces with family problems. A person with problems can be a danger to the others around them in a military situation. Without knowing all the circumstances, I felt Dad could have gotten a hardship transfer and come to our rescue. I was spiraling downward into depression. I finally called Dad and learned Alice had lost her baby. This was very sad news to me. Dad was depressed. I sent a card to Alice expressing my condolences, but I wanted to know exactly what had happened, so I called Bonnie to find out.

Bonnie told me Alice had lost the baby a few days earlier and that it had to do with the delivery channel being too small. The baby had died, but still had to be delivered via a C-section. Bonnie told me that after the stillborn baby boy was delivered, she had stayed with Alice at the hospital. Alice had just sat in a rocking chair holding the baby.

Several days passed when I called Dad to see how things were progressing since the death of the baby. Alice answered the phone with a voice sounding happy and cheerful. When I told her it was I, she jumped all over me, giving me the impression I was guilty of something terrible. Her normal control was gone. She said that Bonnie had told her I said it was sick for a person to sit and hold a dead stillborn child. I was flabbergasted. Nothing I said would change her mind. She wanted to believe Bonnie.

Why in the world would Bonnie tell Alice such a thing? Alice recounted the conversation to me. I denied ever having said such a thing. My anger was beginning to get the best of me. Why did I have to defend myself from false accusations?

After this conversation, I felt it best that I back off from the family for awhile. Some of my friends advised me to give Dad a chance to follow through on his pledge to call me. While my heart was aching to have a family, I would have to wait for a promise that might bear no fruit.

Three months went by, and my forty-fourth birthday came. I felt enough time had passed for Dad to call. I was tired of waiting on someone else to fulfill his or her promise. During this time of mental anguish, Frank Roupas of Roanoke, Virginia gave me much needed moral support. We kept in touch both by phone and letter for one and a half years. As soon as I gave Frank the news about Dad living in Norfolk, his gears began turning. He volunteered to make the five-hour drive from Roanoke to Norfolk to check Dad out. I told him it wasn't necessary. Frank was always sad when he asked me if Pau Pau, his Greek name for my father, had called, and I told him no. He wanted me to come see him when I went back East to meet the family.

There were others who gave me support as well, and I would like to take this opportunity to thank them. I wish I could mention each and every one of their names. Their kindness helped get me through this tough time.

Despite the support given me by friends, my anger toward the family grew during this period. The anger nearly kept me from going. The desire to finish the last chapters of this book was the only motivation remaining to drive me toward a meeting with this side of my family. I had given up any hope of a warm, loving reunion.

I called Dad at six-thirty, Eastern Time, on the sixth of August and was surprised when he answered singing a love song. Obviously, he was expecting his girlfriend to call. When he finally realized it was me he apologized and I asked him if the first of October would be a good time to meet the family. He said that it was. He didn't know it, but I was going regardless of how he reacted.

There was no offer to help with the expenses or even an inquiry as to whether I would be able to foot the bill alone. In fact, there was no offer of a place to stay upon my arrival. I felt frustrated beyond hope.

During the months of waiting, my mood swings were incredible. Some of the time I wanted it all to be over with. Other times I wanted the anticipation to stretch out forever. Mom and Stella invaded my thoughts constantly. I wondered time and time again why I was going through with this meeting with a family that didn't seem to care about me at all. I spent much of my time avoiding life by sleeping and tanning myself in the warm California sun.

Frank Roupas was in constant communication with me. He held me up when I fell. He made me feel that the trip would be worth it just to see him. We were like two little kids plotting and planning my visit there. Of course, I would meet with Frank. He insisted on making plans to meet me at the airport when I arrived.

Not one to be unprepared, I arranged with the media to also be at the airport. Some were receptive to my plans; others were not. My hometown paper, The Modesto Bee, had lost interest in the story and did not want to do a follow up on me meeting Dad unless the local paper in Norfolk did a story. The largest local paper in Norfolk, The Virginia Star Ledger, expressed interest, but in the end did not show up and did not print anything about the reunion. However, the local television station, WAVY, Channel 10, was receptive to covering the event and did show up. I felt the coverage was needed because of this book. I wasn't sure how Dad would take to it, he wasn't told. I was afraid if he knew of the coverage he, like Uncle Charlie, would run.

In addition to lining up the media, I visited my local congressman, Gary Condit, and tried to arrange a meeting with Al Gore and a trip to visit the Congress of the United States. I also sent a letter to Vice President Gore in an effort to meet him face to face. The reason for this was that Vice President Gore was from Tennessee, and his father had been a Tennessee politician. I wanted to draw attention to the need for adoption reform. I failed in my objective to meet with the Vice President, but Congressman Condit did arrange tickets for me to visit the Congress.

I tried to talk Kathy into coming with me. Every card I had was played in that effort. Kathy pummeled me with excuses. I even used the Lee Deboise sales technique I had learned as an Army Reserve Recruiter. She wouldn't bite. She just didn't care to go.

The stage was now set but not everything had been arranged to my satisfaction, as usual. All I had left was to wait until it was time to get on the plane. That waiting proved to be the most difficult thing I have ever done. Ask Ira about it. We had a falling out at this time that nearly destroyed our friendship and our efforts on this book. Fortunately, we patched things up, but I still had the waiting before me and I was born impatient even though I was overdue.

CHAPTER TWENTY TWO
The Triumph

The King of Angels has once again drawn the child back to him. The evil of man dead, the sweet young voice sings again and He listens.

Once again, I loaded up my portable valuables and stowed them at Karen's house as I had done a year earlier before going to Memphis. Karen had prepared a good-bye dinner for me, and we spent a wonderful evening together. There was no long good-bye kiss this time, but then there wasn't a train at my back ready to leave. Karen once again loaned me her luggage. Another sweet lady, Loretta Wallace, also loaned me luggage. I went home to pack.

My flight was scheduled to leave at 10 PM on September 30 from SF International Airport. Carol Boman Geiger and her son Jeremy, also known as the "Jerminator," drove me to the airport. As we sped west on the freeway to San Francisco, Selene (the Greek word for the moon) rose behind us like a giant orange. Carol had worked all day, and I could tell she was tired. If Jeremy hadn't gone with us, I would have made other transportation arrangements. Carol was so nice to drive me to the airport. For this act of compassion, I will forever love her. She is a peach without rival.

Hastily, I smoked one cigarette after another. Not having the benefit of the numbing effects of alcohol, I was stressed to the max. Only my resolve got me through. A drunk standing in line behind me bobbed and weaved as the line moved forward. I could smell his breath several feet away. I hoped he didn't have a bomb in his suitcase. "If we go down," I thought, "he won't feel a thing." I thought back to the many times I had irritated people in my past airplane trips.

I had called each of my children before I left San Francisco. I didn't know if it would be my last call to them or not. If it did turn out to be my last call, they would remember me as a father thinking of them until the end. No doubt about it, I was feeling paranoid as well as stressed. My personal doomsayer was working overtime.

Once on the plane, the fear of flying burst into full bloom. One doesn't really experience the full fear until the plane begins to leave the ground. That is the time that the big jet makes the most noise and the whole plane begins to vibrate as the pilot gives the engines full throttle and pulls back on the stick. My heart beat so fast, I thought I was going to have a heart attack.

To take my mind off my fear, I spent most of the trip speaking with the passengers who would listen to my story and to the stewardesses who were exceptionally receptive. In this way I kept my fear bottled up without having to resort to the bottle.

We landed at Dulles International, Washington, D.C., at six am Eastern Time. The sun was rising in the east as we taxied past a sleek Concord parked on the tarmac. The morning was cold and clear. Through the window, people could be seen scurrying about bundled up in heavy coats, hats and gloves. Heavy condensation was pouring from their facial orifices like frozen flames.

The layover was supposed to last about three hours. At 9 am I was to board a twin engine plane for the last leg of my journey to Norfolk. We disembarked from the jet and sought the warmth of the lounge. There I made the acquaintance of a federal civil servant that had just returned from San Francisco. We swapped stories until nearly time for the plane to leave. Despite this welcome diversion, the emotional tide within me began to rise to flood stage. I smoked cigarette after cigarette and drank several cups of coffee. Not having slept on the plane, I began to feel exhaustion setting in as well.

One hour before my plane was to depart the rising tide of emotion pushed aside the fears of flying. I was less worried about taking off in a twin engine than the jet because if there is trouble in a twin engine, it is light enough to glide to a landing. What did bother me was the reception that awaited me. Would things go smoothly? Would the family be there? Would WAVY be there as they said they would? Would Frank Roupas be there as well? Would Dad be there?

The bombshell hit at 9 am. We were supposed to leave at that time for the forty-minute flight down the coast to Norfolk. We were advised that the plane's departure would be delayed. I felt several megatons of anger inside me ready to blow in an instant.

Our plane was in full sight, parked on the tarmac outside the lounge window. What was the problem here? Had the flight crew slept in? Had they been kidnapped by terrorists? Didn't they know I was to meet my dad at 9:50 am in Norfolk? Didn't they know the media and every one else had been advised of this timing, so crucial to my plans?

Forty-four years worth of anger erupted from within me. I marched on the ticket attendants attacking them with all the fervor of an Islamic Fundamentalist on a Jihad. We were going to leave on time if I had to fly the plane. The ticket attendants were told the story of my life in three minutes. They had to find an alternate way to get me there on time before every one left thinking I had chickened out. Despite the desperate nature of my pleas and the unreasonableness I exhibited, security did not arrive to shoot me with a dart loaded with Thorazine. Instead, the ticket attendants treated me gently with several psychological ploys designed to calm irate passengers such as myself. My anger was stolen from me, but the frustration remained.

At last we boarded the plane for a fifteen-minute wait for the crew. What seemed ages later, we took off. I passed the time telling my story to the other passengers and the stewardesses as I had on the previous flight.

Before leaving Modesto, I had devised a plan for the scene about to take place. I would sit quietly waiting for the last passenger to leave. I knew we would have to cross the tarmac, since commuter planes are not afforded jet walks. And I prayed. When the stewardess told me it was time to go, I would stand up, pat myself down, take a deep breath and say, "It's showtime!"

Our plane began its descent. To our left, the Atlantic Ocean sparkled. The naval shipyards were

on our right. I looked like hell and felt exhausted. At
this point I didn't care. The plane banked to port with
Norfolk Airport dead ahead. Would this crate land
safely or would it crash moments before landing? I
glanced around the cabin. All eyes seemed to be on
me. I smiled back nervously.

After landing, we taxied to the plane's parking spot. The hatch door sprang open and the cold
morning air rushed in to greet us. Was this a portent
of things to come? The other passengers walked by
thanking the stewardess for a safe and pleasant flight.
When all had departed, the stewardess turned to me
and said, "George, you are the last one. It's time to
go."

I grabbed my black and gold briefcase, com-
pliments of my sister, Kathy, and hefted the recently
bought camcorder. The weight of forty-four years
made my movements laborious. I moved as if I was
caught in a planeload of Jello. Suddenly, my adrenaline surged through me like a flash flood. My body
straightened, I patted down the wrinkles in my clothing and I was ready. "It's showtime," I said firmly,
just as I had planned, and walked down the stairs on
feet as light as feathers.

When my feet first touched the tarmac, I noticed that all the other passengers had disappeared. I

was faced with two possibilities for entering the terminal. One of the ground crew, seeing my momentary confusion, directed me to the proper door. I entered the terminal and began to climb the blind concrete stairwell before me. Halfway up I impulsively yelled at the top of my lungs, "Brother Frank, where are you? It's me, Brother Georgie. Where are you big brother Frank? You'd better be there waiting for little Georgie."

I reached the top step, turned to my left and dropped my briefcase and camcorder without thinking of the fragility of electronic instruments. A large, handsome man with no hair put his loving arms around me. I was engulfed in his embrace. I now understand the feeling of security woman experiences when hugged by a man. I hugged Frank back as best as I could. His face was filled with tears of joy as was mine. "We did it," I said. "You called Brother Frankie's name first," Frank said over and over. Then he whispered in my ear, "Your Pau Pau is over here."

I turned my stressed frame to face my father. I couldn't spot him at first, there were so many people milling around. Dad was also very short. There was a cameraman from Channel 10, WAVY, Norfolk, VA, running around with a large TV camera and light accompanied by an attractive young lady who was directing a microphone at me. People were everywhere. Frank walked a few more steps with me then let me go. As he did, a short stout figure emerged from the crowd with tears pouring down his cheeks. Without uttering a word, I grabbed Dad like a man clinging to dear life. I was oblivious to all except that I now held my father in my arms. My thoughts rushed through my head like fallen leaves dancing on the wind, and the tears fell down my cheeks like a gentle rain after a season of drought.

My arms sensed a pair of gnarly shoulders. These were the shoulders of a man who worked hard all his life. He had spent most of his life in the merchant marines where hard work is a must. As I held on to him, I reflected on my first sight of him standing in the crowd with his head bowed and eyes cast straight down. His entire life must have been guilt ridden because of what happened to his children. Now, he would have a chance to heal.

Our eyes finally met. He gazed up at me. Those eyes of his said, "I'm sorry son. I can't change the past, but I can make a difference now." However, his first words to me were, "You're taller than me!" All I could do was laugh and try to forgive him. "You're right, I am," I replied.

He guided me toward Alice, my beautiful half-sister and Aunt Stella who was even shorter than Dad. We all hugged and kissed. Stella introduced me to Charlie, my cousin. How ironic that both sides of the family would have an Aunt Stella and a cousin Charlie! This cousin Charlie was the antithesis of cousin Charlie Kirk. He was younger looking than his years, and he shook my hand like the proper gentleman he is. I could tell by his smile that he was an unflappable individual and a real character. His grin was mischievous like he had done something wrong and gotten away cleanly.

Next, came Johnny, Stella's oldest son. The eyes that peeked out from his fully bearded face spoke little of the person within. Dad then prepared to introduce me to his wife, Bonnie. Lisa Parker, the reporter from WAVY, Channel 10, interrupted him. She was very gently trying to rig me with a small clip-on microphone on the inside of my shirt where it wouldn't show. I smiled approvingly.

When I turned back to the family, Bonnie was standing there before me, beautiful and radiant. Bunky, the name I came to know her by, appeared as if she had stepped out of the pages of Glamour Magazine. She was three months younger than I. After our introduction; she assured me our last conversation on the phone was just a gross misunderstanding. I took her comments at face value, but I made a mental note to keep an eye on her, just in case.

I wondered what it was that they had expected to see when I arrived. Had they thought they would be confronted with a wounded animal looking for forty-four years of revenge? Had they felt intimidated by my sudden appearance from the mists of time, a possible rival for Dad's affection and their inheritances? Or had they expected what they got, a man joyful at seeing his family for the first time ever? I suddenly found myself wishing my sister, Kathy, had been with me to share this moment of triumph.

A friend of Dad's, Dave Hoviak, made a copy of the video shown on the evening news for me. Wanting to save every precious moment of our meeting I could, I requested a copy of the makeup tape from WAVY and offered to defray the cost to the station. I never received this copy, but this event is etched in my memory not to be forgotten in the shuffle of every day life. After returning home, I sent Lisa a thank-you card for covering the event. About the same time, I received a note from Lisa restating the policy of the station and apologizing for not being able to do more. She had stated it to me upon my first request of the tape.

We retrieved my luggage and exited the terminal. Out into the bright morning sunlight we went. The exhilaration of meeting Dad coupled with the brisk morning air brought the color to my cheeks. Every one piled into their cars. We were at Dad's place in about eight minutes. Lisa and her camera-man were part of the cavalcade.

We entered The Stonehouse through the back door and passed through the poolroom. Two well kept tables sat quietly, knowing they would be well used later that evening. We moved on into the restaurant area and through the bar. Overall, Dad runs a very tidy, tasteful operation. I was pleased and impressed with his ability to create and run such a place.

I couldn't help but notice the similarities be-tween Dad's place and mine. Sitting on his bar were two ceramic statues, one of an owl and the other a lion. Sister Kathy has a large owl collection in her home, and I have a collection of lions. There were two lava lamps, one red, the other blue, decorating his bar. I have a red lava lamp prominently displayed in my home. There was a black cat; a friendly little stray Dad takes care of. I love cats, too. I have two of them and they are as friendly as Dad's.

There were other similarities between us as well. Even though Dad is sixty-eight, he has a great build. If I hadn't known his age, I would have guessed him to be several years younger. I have always taken pride in my build and in keeping fit. I, too, look younger than my years. I have a mustache like my dad's, and both of us have well manicured hands. We both have been in business. In addition, every one kept saying how much we look alike, although at first, I didn't agree with this last part.

On Friday and Saturday nights, Dad has a disc jockey come in to play music for his patrons. The dance area doubles as his banquet facility. What an excellent arrangement! "You're a smart man," I told Dad when I saw how well he had put his business together. "You're right, son," he replied. No humility there! I was reminded of myself.

The kitchen belongs to Dad, but over the door leading into it is a sign that says, "Edith's Kitchen." Edith is a beautiful lady who has been with Dad forever. She has worked with him so long, they both think alike. During my stay, she and Moniqué, her assistant, made me feel very much at home. Whenever they saw me they would ask if I were hungry. If I were, they would whip up a fabulous dish of something for me to eat. Both are great cooks. Dad was the same way. He was always asking, "Are you hungry, son?" I wanted to be hungry all the time just so I could hear him call me "son" over and over. It sounded so wonderful after such a long and torturous wait. It took me awhile, but I came to realize that Dad and his side of the family have a kind of love, but they are also distanced from each other much in the same way my sister and I are distanced, despite living in the same town. My mind finds this concept difficult to accept, but I love Dad, and I accept him as he is. During my visit with him, he showed me love and understanding as well as acceptance.

I had a strong desire to go behind the bar and play bartender. I had the feeling I would meet a few of the local ladies that way, and I did. Two of the female bartenders, without coming right out and saying it, informed me that, boss's son or not, I was to stay out from behind the bar when they were working.

Dad checked me into the Econo Lodge Motel directly across the Old Military Highway from "The Stonehouse." The highway is a four-lane road that takes a badge of courage to cross in the daylight due to the high volume of traffic. The manager of the motel was an affable man with a heavy Indian accent. Upon my arrival there the first night, he informed me that Dad would pay all my expenses, including my phone calls while I stayed there. Thank

you Dad. I love you. The manager had seen the news-
cast of our meeting, and he was elated for both of us.
Every day he would be there at the office to wave to
me as I prepared to cross the highway to "The
Stonehouse." I always waved ·back, and we exchanged broad smiles.

Dad helped me with many things while I was
there. He made me feel at home and at ease. At one
point I jokingly asked him if he could fix me up with
a girl. His reply was, "You have to take care of that
yourself." He exhibited a great deal of wisdom in
this statement. I wish I had known him much longer
than I have. I feel that despite the distance he keeps
between his relatives and himself, and despite the
attention his business receives from him, I would
have benefited greatly from knowing this man better. It is too bad things couldn't have worked out that
way.

I wanted to use my tickets to visit The White
House and to see Congress. My hope was to connect
with someone who would be able to help in my cru-
sade to change the adoption laws. Unfortunately, the
bus schedules did not match with my schedule. I
needed to rent a car. That was not possible due to the
lack of credit and credit card. Dad came to my rescue by loaning me his card to get a car so I could go

to the nation's Capitol.

My trip was uneventful. I made no contacts as I had envisioned, but I did get to tour Assemblyman Gary Condit's office and the Congress where I sat in the Speaker's chair for a brief moment. I did not make it to The White House due to the long lines of people waiting to get in.

When I returned to Norfolk, I spent the evening with Dad beginning with a delicious dinner. Over dinner, I learned that Stevie Ray Vaughn used to drop by Dad's to play his guitar, before he made it big. It seems Dad had lots of surprises for me to discover in his life. I wish I could have stayed longer to discover more about him.

I asked Dad if I could borrow his wife the next day. We both had a chuckle over that! Bunky and I wanted to spend the day together at Virginia Beach. I wanted to visit the Association for Research and Enlightenment and the Edgar Casey Foundation. In any case, we went with my dad's blessing. It's not often a guy can spend the day with his "mom" who is three months younger than he is. We had a lot of fun with that. Bunky turned out to be not only beautiful, but charming as well. My earlier feelings of anxiety towards her due to the unfortunate misunderstanding over our phone conversation dissolved that day. We had a great time together and wound it all up with Bunky buying me lunch.

I realize now that the days preceding my meeting with Dad were filled with suspicion and paranoia. The stress I had put myself under intensified the situation. I had forgotten my vow not to let circumstances lull me into setting goals too high to be reached. After setting those impossibly high goals, I felt the screws tighten every time it seemed a wrench was thrown into the works of my plans. Stress is a silent, lethal killer.

My life has been like a puzzle with the pieces strewn all over the place. I took forty years to find all the pieces and put them together. I am so glad I met Dad. Perhaps I am disappointed by his distant behavior, but I cannot take it personally because that is the way Dad is with all the family. While on my stay, I found out much about the man. Most of it made me proud to be his son. One thing I did learn is that he loves me, and I love him and I love to hear him call me "son." That is all that matters in the whole world.

My time to leave came all too soon. With hugs, kisses and warm tears from Dad, Bunky, and myself, I departed on a plane and found my way back to Modesto and my life here. I hope to see my relatives on both sides of the family again. I would like them all to meet my sister and my son, Andrew, and daughter Jennifer. There are lots of things I want in regards to my family. The most important thing, however, has been accomplished. I now know the joy of having a family, of sharing their love, of knowing who I am. Dear God, thank you for allowing your child, George Curtis, this great triumph in his life.

CHAPTER TWENTY THREE
After The Dust Had Cleared

After my return home, I had some time to think about all that had happened in my life. I also ran into a person doing some very important research which I will tell you about later.

School was very difficult for me in every way conceivable. Switching schools frequently didn't help. One of the problems that made it so difficult had to do with my glasses. I went through pair after pair of glasses that were broken or lost. The punishment I received for losing or breaking them aside, the glasses have turned out to be a miss-diagnosis. The glasses were a constant source of pain for me in the physical sense. They made my head hurt. My problems in school were diagnosed as a vision problem, hence the glasses. Some of my symptoms were; easily distracted, failure to stay on task, avoidance of assignments, low self-esteem, and poor language skills.

After I was fitted with glasses, there were several years where no improvement was noticeable. I only had one ally to help me through, my third grade teacher, Mrs. Rydell. She would break into tears, God bless her, as she held me. She knew I was intelligent and something was wrong. Yes, something was wrong. I was dyslexic. This I recently discovered through tests administered by a friend of mine whose life has been devoted to the study of dyslexia.

I recently read, "The Brilliant Idiot", an autobiography of Abraham Schmidt. He chronicled his experiences as a dyslexic growing up. His story was similar to mine. We were both victims of a learning disorder that wouldn't be researched until the seventies. We were both viewed as individuals who did not try hard enough. We were both pitted against our teachers who thought it was a test of wills that was going on in their classroom. The best analogy to our experience is for the reader of this book to pick up another book written in Chinese and try to understand what is being said.

I was given Geratol in elementary school in order to boost my energy level and thereby improve my schoolwork. It wasn't successful. Neither were the beatings I received from John.

I had problems learning in the military. I was frustrated. I knew I was smart, so why wasn't I able to read better? Slowly, I began to develop strategies to cope with my learning problems. I wanted to go to college after I got out of the service to prove I was smart and not stupid. I needed to prove it to myself as well as the Bubnes family and every one else in my life.

Upon my arrival at college, I was immediately put on academic probation. My grade point average in Junior College dropped to 1.98. It was a struggle, but I managed to raise it barely over the 2.0 needed to stay in school. I barely graduated with my Associate of Arts degree and my Bachelor of Arts degree, but I did do what I set out to do.

I recently met an intelligent and beautiful woman, Judy Littlefield. She is a school trained dyslexia screener. She is a dyslexic, as are two of her children. Her son Robbie, and daughter's Robyn and Jennifer, are very special to me. During the daytime she is a highly successful high school resource teacher, and she recently completed her Masters Degree. Her Thesis, "Dyslexia and Alcoholism," is fascinating. Her wish is to study the correlation of dyslexia with alcoholism. She is the one who tested me for dyslexia and found me to be positive. There is a strong probability that my children are also dyslexic. Studies are showing that dyslexia is genetic especially in families that carry the genetic propensity to addiction.

During the evolution of the study of this disorder, much progress has been made with much more being needed. During the fifties, very little information was available. This was rough on me and anyone else with the same condition. How could I read the eye charts at the optometrist's office correctly when I had dyslexia? I was given eyeglasses that hurt my eyes to correct the perceived problem. The sad part is that this is still going on. Glasses will not correct a problem that is not visual but is centered in the language processing center of the brain. The Orton Society has estimated that as much as twenty per cent of all Americans are dyslexic.

The myth about dyslexics that has to be expunged is that our mental abilities will hold us back from achieving any academic success above a high school diploma. At the end of his autobiography, Mr. Schmidt was given an I. Q. test. Please remember that for a dyslexic to take such a test without knowledge of their condition would make the test worthless. Mr. Schmidt tested in the top two- percent. Dyslexics typically score high on intelligence tests in later years.

What we need to do is to identify those children in our school systems that have this learning disorder. By practicing intervention, we will be saving the schools and society a lot of headaches. As it stands, we are spending much more by waiting until the children are placed in special education classes where they are stigmatized and develop low self-esteem. School budgets are presently strained with the growing special education student body. We could save so much money and so much pain by testing early and intervening early to correct the problem. I am positive this would also save some space in our prisons.

I recently spoke to the people at the Stanislaus Superintendents Office. There are 124,000 students, K-12 in the county. Of these, there are approximately 10,000 special education students. These are students who have been identified as having a minimum of one standard deviation from the norm. How many of them are dyslexic?

Using the Orton Society's minimum of fifteen percent of the population criteria, out of 124,000 students, one would expect to find about 18,000 dyslexics. Without the proper testing and placement of these students, we can safely say that they are being shafted.

As badly as this country needs National Adoption Reform legislation, it is equally incumbent upon us to reform our educational processes as well. Dyslexia screening should be a part of it. If we are to continue as a successful nation, we must tend to the needs and rights of our children.

CHAPTER TWENTY FOUR
The Right To Know

Our country's policies are shaped around the principle of reaction—something happens, and we react to it. Very often we do not react with the correct solution. The problem is that we do not plan for problems until they happen to meet the media's criteria for scandal of the hour. By the time legislation is proposed to correct the problem, it has only become yesterday's problem having dropped from sight of the public. The legislation often only addresses the gut feelings of the general public opinion as to the best course of action, not necessarily the best course to take.

The problem is that our welfare state and the adoption secrecy laws are promoting promiscuity and irresponsibility. Our children are having children, which is OK because Daddy Sam will send minimal support, thus absolving the two individuals of the responsibility of the life they have created. If this is not acceptable to the individuals involved, they can put the child up for adoption and the second the surrender papers are signed, wash their hands completely of the life they have created. The secrecy laws allow these "parents" to remain anonymous and to escape responsibility for their acts. What is more, the children conceived in this manner and adopted out are deprived of the knowledge of where they came from. They are deprived of the ability to confront their biological parents and to learn about their real heritage both in a genetic and a historical sense.

Too many of our children have limited choices these days, choices they are not able to make. A child, once conceived by an irresponsible set of parents, may be aborted, adopted, or raised on welfare. The irresponsible parents make the choice. Is this fair to the children?

Perhaps stronger incentives to act responsibly are needed. If a child is put up for adoption, the biological parents should be made to contribute to the support of that child even if they never see the child again. The support should last until the child reaches legal adulthood. Any time after that, the child should have access to their adoption files so that they may be able to find out who they are and where they came from if they choose. To most of us, identity is everything.

There should also be disincentives for people on welfare to have children. The true test of prospective parenthood should not be how fertile you are. It should be based instead on the parents' ability to raise and provide for the child they have conceived.

Children are now sexually active at earlier ages, yet many of them are not being taught to be responsible for themselves or their actions. Our welfare system encourages irresponsibility. We have to take responsibility for them until such time as they are able to learn how to be responsible.

A change in the secrecy laws is a start. Do we not all have the right to know who we are and what our origins were? Once a child is adopted, there should be some checks made to be sure that child is being taken care of properly. Both the child's physical and emotional life should be checked on. The laws have to apply to all states equally so that all children have equal protection. This is important. Our children are important. The right to know is important.

I have said this before, and I will say it again, our children are the most important part of our future. Our children are the future. If we do not take care of our children, there will be no future.

I recently contacted a public official whose specialty is adoptions. He was a very nice man and well versed on the issues concerning babies for profit. What he told me really shocked me. The amount of money involved in selling babies would make Tann and Kelley roll over in their graves. A healthy, white male newborn commands a price of $50,000.

Currently there are two avenues of adoption, public and private. Public adoptions fall under the auspices of the county social services. Stanislaus County has one of the highest unemployment rates in the nation. Our welfare rolls are bursting at the seams, yet we have only three Placement Caseworkers in our social services department for the whole county. Is it any wonder private adoptions are flourishing?

The bottom line is that just as Georgia Tann advertised babies for adoption while at the same time taking care that the supply side was well-stocked, entities exist today that do the same thing. Their ads are in our classified pages. They will take care of poor expectant mothers as Tann would and see to it that the children are adopted if the mothers give up custody. Probate court must still be cleared. The child is first legally abandoned and immediately adopted to a waiting family. This all costs money. The adoptive family is expected to pay for it. Do poor people have money to pay for this adoption process? No. Wealthy people do. Does wealth insure a nurturing home for the child? No!

Public adoptions require several home follow-up investigations. In the case of the private adoptions, the child is placed before the state has a chance to approve the paperwork. Home investigations are a sham. It is clear that the TCHS scandal can and is being repeated. And the secrecy laws that helped Tann and Kelley are still in effect hiding these acts and those responsible.

A farmer plants his seed and carefully tends the seedlings knowing that this is the only way to ensure a good crop and to safeguard his future as a farmer. Why can't we do this for our children and our future as a free and viable society?

SALVATION

I came from the darkness
On the way,
I went through hell,
Misery was my name.
Life was not worth living.
The end was at hand.
I was helpless
To change the impending doom.
It was pretty clear,
Life was not for me.
The end did come,
but not as I thought it would.
A strange yet beautiful
Metamorphosis took shape.
The dark was supplanted
With sunshine
The darkness of hell
Became sunbeams from Heaven.
I held out for a hero
And found a God

CHAPTER TWENTY FIVE
A View From the Outside

It was July of 1988 when I first met Brian Bubnes. He was moving into my apartment, and I was
moving in with my brother several blocks away. I
sold him my old beat-up couch with a hide-a-bed in
it. He has been talking about how I bested him in
this deal ever since.

My first impression of Brian was that he was
a strange individual to say the least. I had a very
strong urge to kid him about his name, but being a
polite person, I did not. When I moved back into the
same apartment complex two months later, I found
him at my door constantly. At that time I was thinking of moving to Oregon to put some distance between my ex-wife and myself. I told Brian of this
one day, and he gave me an answer I will never forget: "You can't move to Oregon. You have to stay
here and be my friend."

I realized at the time that this statement was
partly in jest. I now realize that less of it was in jest
than I had originally thought, however. There was a
fragility about this large man standing before me,
despite his size and obnoxious attitude. His vulner-
ability impressed me, and that is why I probably re-

membered his words.

From acquaintance, I went to employee, to friend and onward to business partner. Writing this book together has made us even closer friends than we would otherwise have been. Throughout this adventure I have watched him change before my eyes. The biggest changes took place just after his reunion with his mother's side of the family and after his reunion with his father. This last change was by far the greatest.

Until I united with him in an effort to produce this book, I never quite knew what to think of his search for his family. When he began trying to convince me to help him write the story, I found myself not able to believe some of the things that happened to him. The documentation helped, as did some of the communications I had with some of his newfound relatives. There are parts of the story that were impossible to document, and we just have to take his word that they happened. Most of these incidents occurred in his childhood. Having extensive education in the ways of the world and some education in abnormal behavior, I can tell you that his account of what happened is probably true. He has exhibited personality traits of a person who grew from an abusive childhood. Being his friend and knowing of his sincerity in these matters, I can say that I am convinced it is all true - minus the slight inaccuracies that occur because of his young age when some of the incidents happened. The slight change in perspective, years of time give all of us.

I feel privileged to have worked with George on this project and hope that the goals he has set will be reached. I also hope to work with him on future projects. In the meantime, I want each and every one of you to know that the metamorphosis from Brian to George has been a painful process for this individual. The miracle is that it has happened, and a person I once saw as an obnoxious acquaintance has turned into a self-actualized human being I call friend.

Ira White

Bibliography

Austin, Linda Tollett. Babies For Sale: The Tennessee Children's Home Adoption Scandal. UMI Dissertation Services, 1992.

Glad, Denny. Interviews with author by telephone, 1992-1993.

Glad, Denny. Interview with author in Memphis, March 16, 1992.

Kirk/Curtis Family History, Case Number 6773, copied by the hand of Denny Glad, February 28, 1992.

Miller, Vallie S. Report To J. O. McMahan, Commissioner, Public Welfare, State of Tennessee. June 12, 1951.

Taylor, Robert L. Report to J. O. McMahan, Commissioner of Public Welfare of the State of Tennessee. May 21, 1951.

Printed in the United States
71444LV00001B/1-99

9 780965 830201